Cooking with
Rotisserie
Chicken

A QUICK START TO EASY RECIPES

by Theresa Millang

T0123841

Adventure Publications, Inc.
Cambridge, MN

Thank You

A special thank you goes to friends and family across the country and to all others who contributed to this recipe collection. I have included all my favorite recipes and I hope you will enjoy them as much as I do.

Edited by Dan Downing and Brett Ortler

Book design by Lora Westberg

Cover design by Jonathan Norberg

10 9 8 7 6 5 4 3 2 1

Copyright 2011 by Theresa Nell Millang
Published by Adventure Publications, Inc.
820 Cleveland St. S
Cambridge, MN 55008
1-800-678-7006
www.adventurepublications.net

ISBN: 978-1-59193-317-5

Table of Contents

Introduction

Everyday life can be hectic, and people are constantly looking for fast, easy and healthy ways to prepare homemade food for their families. You can count on *Cooking with Rotisserie Chicken* to help. This collection of recipes features countless ways to use a store-bought rotisserie chicken to prepare a wide variety of meals, including tried-and-true classics and contemporary dishes. The meals in this book are perfect for everyday eating, yet good enough to present to special company. Better yet, most of the recipes in this book can be prepared in 20 minutes of cooking time.

Rotisserie Chicken: Delicious, Healthy and Readily Available

Rotisserie chicken is a favorite at many households in America, and that's no surprise. Meals that incorporate rotisserie chicken are tasty, easy to prepare, and require little planning. Rotisserie chicken is healthy too; it's naturally low in fat, high in protein, and it's delicious. Incorporating rotisserie chicken into a meal couldn't be easier, simply head to the local grocery store, pick up a chicken, and get cooking.

Selection & Storage

Rotisserie chickens come in a variety of sizes, and in addition to plain chicken, there is a range of flavors, including lemon herb, barbecue and garlic. This flavoring rarely goes deeper than the skin; nevertheless, if you prepare your meal with the chicken skin, flavor matters, so take it into consideration.

When purchasing a rotisserie chicken, be sure that it is fresh. Rotisserie chickens are usually kept in heating cases beneath heat lamps. (These cases are often near the cash registers.) If possible, avoid chicken that has been beneath heat lamps for an extended period. In addition, be sure the chicken is hot when you take it from the heating case. (USDA safety guidelines states that all hot foods are to be kept at 140°F or warmer.) If you don't use the chicken immediately, refrigerate the chicken within 2 hours of purchase to prevent spoiling. (Refrigerate it within 1 hour if the air temperature is above 90°F).

The USDA recommends eating rotisserie chicken within 3 to 4 days of purchase. If you do not use the chicken in that time frame, you can freeze the unused pieces for up to 4 months in freezer-quality plastic storage bags or plastic food containers. If you plan to use the chicken in a recipe, remove the meat from the bones and cut it into small pieces (this will also make it easier to store). When thawing frozen chicken, always keep the chicken in the refrigerator, never on the counter.

Carving a Rotisserie Chicken

First, get out a sharp knife—a carving knife or similar long-bladed knife works best. Place the chicken on a cutting board, breast side up. Remove each wing by cutting through the joint between the wing and the breast while using your other hand to hold the wing away from the body. To remove the thighs and legs, cut between the thigh and the body while gently pulling the leg and thigh away, to help reveal the joint. Cut through the joint to separate the thigh from the chicken. Cut the leg from the thigh by slicing through the connecting joint.

To make thin slices from the breast, such as meat for sandwiches, make a deep horizontal cut into the breast just above the wing joint. Next, cut downward to the horizontal cut, working from the outer edge of the breast to the center.

If you want to cut out the entire chicken breast, feel where the breast meat attaches to the chicken and cut along the bone. This will enable you to remove the breast in two halves.

Boneless Chicken Equivalents

1 average whole chicken = 3 cups

White meat only = 2 cups

Dark meat only = 1 cup

Appetizers

Chicken and Black Bean Quesadillas

INGREDIENTS

1 cup shredded rotisserie chicken, skin removed
⅔ cup sour cream
⅓ cup mayonnaise
¼ cup sliced green onions
1 ½ cups shredded Cheddar cheese
1 15-ounce can black beans, rinsed and drained
2 tablespoons chopped green chiles, drained
12 (8-inch) flour tortillas
2 tablespoons butter, melted

Toppings
Sour cream
Salsa
Guacamole
Chopped olives
Sliced green onions
Chopped fresh tomatoes

36 APPETIZERS

Preheat oven to 375°.

1 Mix the first seven ingredients in a large bowl to make filling. Spread about ¼ cup filling on half of each tortilla. Fold tortilla in half to cover filling. Brush both sides of each tortilla with butter.

2 Place filled tortillas onto ungreased baking sheets. Bake 10 to 15 minutes or until heated through. Cut each quesadilla into 3 wedges. Serve as desired with topping ingredients. Refrigerate leftovers.

These appetizers are sure to be a party pleaser!

 Variation: Serve for lunch with a green salad and fruit.

Ki Ki's Microwave Chicken Nachos

1 For each serving, arrange about 2 cups tortilla chips in a single layer on a microwave-safe serving plate. Sprinkle evenly with cheese. Top evenly with shredded chicken, then sprinkle with more cheese.

2 Microwave on high about 20 seconds or until cheese is just melting.

3 Serve immediately, topped as desired, with tomatoes, green onions, avocado, sour cream and salsa. Refrigerate leftovers.

My friend Ki Ki lives in beautiful Minnesota, and shares this appetizer recipe.

Variation: Heat a 15-ounce can of refried beans with 2 tablespoons taco seasoning in a saucepan. Top tortillas with mixture, then continue as above.

INGREDIENTS

8 cups sturdy white tortilla chips
2 cups shredded Cheddar cheese, divided
2 cups shredded rotisserie chicken, skin removed

Toppings
Diced fresh tomatoes
Sliced green onions
Diced avocado
Sour cream
Salsa

4 APPETIZERS

Mango Chicken Canapés

INGREDIENTS

2 (2.1-ounce) boxes frozen mini
   phyllo shells
1 cup chilled chopped rotisserie
   chicken, skin removed
½ cup chopped fresh mango
3½ tablespoons light Oriental
   dressing
1½ tablespoons Thai peanut
   satay sauce
2 tablespoons thinly sliced
   green onions
1 tablespoon chopped fresh cilantro

30 APPETIZERS

Preheat oven to 350°.

1 Place phyllo shells on a baking sheet and crisp in the oven for 2 to 4 minutes; cool.

2 Stir together remaining ingredients and spoon into shells.

 Tip: Purchased phyllo cups make short work of these appetizers.

Mini Waffles with Chicken

1 Stir chicken, cheese and barbecue sauce in a medium-sized microwave-safe bowl; microwave on high 1 to 1½ minutes to warm.

2 Toast waffles in the toaster until lightly browned; top each with chicken mixture. Sprinkle with green onions as desired; serve. Refrigerate leftovers.

Variation: Spread toasted waffles with cream cheese, then add chicken mixture.

INGREDIENTS

1½ cups finely chopped rotisserie chicken, skin removed
2 cups shredded sharp Cheddar cheese
¾ cup barbecue sauce, your choice of flavor
1 10.9-ounce package mini waffles
Chopped green onion

40 APPETIZERS

Mini Wonton Quiches

INGREDIENTS

24 wonton wrappers (3¼x3 inches)
4 eggs
1 tablespoon all-purpose flour
¼ teaspoon salt
⅛ teaspoon black pepper
3 tablespoons finely chopped
    rotisserie chicken, skin removed
3 tablespoons finely chopped
    fully cooked ham
2 tablespoons finely chopped
    green onion
2 tablespoons finely chopped
    red bell pepper

2 DOZEN QUICHES

Preheat oven to 350°.

1 Coat 24 muffin cups with cooking spray.

2 Gently press 1 wonton wrapper into each cup, allowing ends to extend above edges.

3 Beat eggs and flour in a medium bowl until blended. Stir in remaining ingredients. Spoon about ½ tablespoon mixture into each wonton-lined muffin cup.

4 Bake in center of oven until filling is set, about 12 to 15 minutes. Remove from muffin cups to a wire rack. Serve. Refrigerate leftovers.

Serve these little appetizers with sweet and sour sauce and hot mustard.

Pesto Chicken Tomatoes

1 Remove seeds from each tomato half with a small spoon. Discard seeds.

2 Stir remaining ingredients in a medium bowl; spoon equal amounts of mixture into each tomato. Refrigerate. Serve chilled. Refrigerate leftovers.

Make these appetizers several hours before ready to serve; refrigerate.

 Tip: Roma tomatoes are the firm Italian tomatoes usually used for making sauce.

INGREDIENTS

12 fresh ripe baby Roma tomatoes, halved lengthwise
½ cup finely chopped rotisserie chicken, skin removed
2 tablespoons pesto, purchased or homemade
2 tablespoons shredded Asiago cheese

24 SMALL APPETIZERS

Summer Spring Rolls with Asian Dipping Sauce

INGREDIENTS

Half of a 3.75-ounce package
    cellophane noodles
1 12-ounce package spring
    roll wrappers
1 10-ounce head Boston lettuce,
    leaves separated
¾ cup coarsely grated carrot
¾ cup very thinly cut English
    cucumber strips
2 cups shredded rotisserie chicken
    breast, skin removed
½ cup coarsely chopped cilantro
½ cup very thinly cut 1-inch-long
    green onion strips
⅓ cup very thinly cut radish strips

Dipping Sauce
½ cup rice wine vinegar
½ cup granulated sugar
2 tablespoons oyster sauce
2 teaspoons soy sauce
1 teaspoon minced garlic
1 teaspoon sesame oil
¼ teaspoon crushed red pepper flakes
1 sliced green onion

16 ROLLS

1 Soak noodles in hot water for 15 minutes; drain well and snip into 2-inch lengths. Keep covered with moist paper towel. Remove 16 spring roll wrappers. Dip one wrapper in warm water for 5 seconds, then remove and arrange between 2 moist paper towels. Repeat with remaining wrappers. Do not stack.

2 Remove top towel from one wrapper. Top with lettuce leaf, leaving 1 inch on sides. Layer with $\frac{1}{16}$ of carrot, cucumber, chicken and a ¼-inch bundle of noodles. Top with $\frac{1}{16}$ of cilantro, onion and radish.

3 Starting with wrapper edge nearest you, fold edge up about 2 inches. Fold each end just to cover filling, then continue to roll. Repeat steps 2 and 3 with remaining ingredients.

4 Place spring rolls in a 9x13-inch baking pan. Cover with moist paper towel and plastic wrap; refrigerate up to 3 hours. To serve, bring rolls to room temperature (no more than one hour out of refrigeration). Cut spring rolls in half diagonally. Serve with dipping sauce. Refrigerate leftovers.

Dipping Sauce
1 Combine sauce ingredients in a bowl. Mix well.

Serve these special appetizers to special friends.

Breakfast
& Brunch

Breakfast Pizza

INGREDIENTS

1 8-ounce package frozen brown-and-serve pork sausage links, cut into ½-inch pieces
½ tablespoon corn oil
6 eggs, beaten
4 (6-inch) ready-to-serve pizza crusts
½ cup shredded Cheddar cheese, divided
1 cup shredded rotisserie chicken breast, skin removed
4 slices crisply cooked bacon, crumbled

4 SERVINGS

Preheat oven to 400°.

1 Spray a 10-inch nonstick skillet with cooking spray; heat over medium heat. Add sausage to skillet; cook about 3 minutes, stirring occasionally until brown; drain. Remove sausage from skillet; set aside.

2 Heat corn oil in same skillet. Pour beaten eggs into skillet. When mixture begins to set at bottom and side, gently lift cooked portions with a spatula so that the thin, uncooked portion can flow to bottom. Do not stir. Cook 4 to 5 minutes or until eggs are thickened through but still moist.

3 Place pizza crusts on ungreased baking sheets. Sprinkle each equally with half the cheese. Top each with egg, sausage, chicken and bacon. Sprinkle each with remaining cheese. Bake about 10 to 12 minutes or until cheese is melted. Serve. Refrigerate leftovers.

Sausage, bacon and chicken are used to make this delicious breakfast treat.

Variation: For brunch, top with diced tomatoes, sliced sautéed mushrooms, sliced green onions or diced green bell pepper before topping with final cheese layer.

Cajun Omelet

1 Melt 1 teaspoon butter in a 10-inch nonstick heavy skillet over medium-high heat. Add sausage; cook and stir until sausage is well browned, about 7 minutes. Add chicken, tomatoes, onion, bell pepper, celery, garlic and ½ teaspoon Creole seasoning. Cook and stir until vegetables are tender and most of liquid has evaporated, about 5 minutes. Remove from skillet. Wipe skillet clean.

2 Whisk eggs, parsley and remaining ½ teaspoon Creole seasoning in a medium bowl.

3 Melt 1 teaspoon butter in skillet over medium heat, rotating pan to evenly coat bottom. Pour one-fourth of egg mixture into skillet. As egg mixture starts to cook, gently lift eggs with a spatula and tilt pan so uncooked portion flows underneath. Cook until almost set, about 1 minute. Cover skillet and cook 1 minute.

4 Sprinkle one side of omelet with one-fourth of sausage mixture and one-fourth of cheese. Fold omelet in half over filling. Slide omelet onto a serving plate; cover with aluminum foil to keep warm. Repeat steps 3 and 4 to make remaining omelets. Serve immediately. Refrigerate leftovers.

Serve this delicious entrée for brunch or a light supper, along with a spinach or baby lettuce salad and warm French bread. Pass the hot sauce!

INGREDIENTS

5 teaspoons butter, divided
¾ cup thinly sliced andouille or chorizo sausage
½ cup finely diced rotisserie chicken breast, skin removed
2 small plum tomatoes, seeded and chopped
½ medium yellow onion, chopped
½ medium red bell pepper, chopped
¼ cup chopped celery
1 teaspoon minced garlic
1 teaspoon Creole seasoning, divided
12 large eggs
1 tablespoon chopped flat leaf parsley
1½ cups shredded Monterey Jack cheese

4 SERVINGS

Chicken Frittata

INGREDIENTS

1 tablespoon margarine
1 medium new red potato, peeled
  and chopped (about ½ cup)
⅓ cup sliced zucchini
⅓ cup sliced yellow onions, rings
  separated
½ cup cubed rotisserie chicken breast,
  skin removed
½ teaspoon dried basil, crumbled
½ teaspoon dried dill weed, crumbled
⅛ teaspoon ground black pepper
1 8-ounce carton frozen egg
  substitute, thawed

4 SERVINGS

1 Spray a 9-inch nonstick skillet with cooking spray. Melt margarine in skillet over medium-low heat.

2 Stir next seven ingredients in a bowl; add to skillet. Cover and cook over medium-low heat until potatoes are almost tender, about 6 minutes, stirring occasionally.

3 Pour egg substitute evenly over mixture in skillet. Cover and cook over medium-low heat 6 minutes. Gently lift cooked portion around edge to allow uncooked portion to flow underneath. Cover and cook until set, about 2½ minutes. Slide onto a heated serving platter. Serve immediately.

Egg substitute is used in this delicious open-faced omelet. Serve with fresh fruit and buttered toast.

Egg and Chicken English Muffin

1 Coat a large nonstick skillet with cooking spray; heat over medium heat until hot.

2 Pour in eggs. As eggs begin to set, gently pull the eggs across the pan with an inverted turner, forming large, soft curds. Continue cooking, pulling, lifting and folding eggs until thickened and no visible liquid egg remains. Do not stir constantly.

3 Spoon eggs equally onto English muffin bottoms. Top each with cheese, chicken and bacon. Cover with muffin tops. Serve. Refrigerate leftovers.

Serve this delightful sandwich for breakfast or lunch.

INGREDIENTS

4 **eggs**, beaten with a pinch of salt and black pepper
4 **English muffins**, split, toasted and buttered
4 slices **American cheese**
4 slices **rotisserie chicken breast**, thinly sliced, skin removed
4 slices **crisp-cooked bacon**

4 SERVINGS

Light Style
Breakfast Wraps

INGREDIENTS

3 eggs
3 egg whites
¼ teaspoon black pepper
⅛ teaspoon salt
1½ cups shredded reduced fat Colby
  Jack cheese, divided
½ cup chopped fully cooked ham
½ cup finely diced rotisserie chicken
  breast, skin removed
¼ cup thinly sliced green onion
¼ teaspoon hot pepper sauce, optional
4 (8-inch) whole wheat flour tortillas or
  flavored wraps, warmed according
  to package directions

4 SERVINGS

1 Beat eggs, egg whites, black pepper and salt in a medium bowl.

2 Stir in 1 cup cheese, ham, chicken, green onion and hot sauce.

3 Coat a large nonstick skillet with cooking spray; place over medium-high heat. Add egg mixture; cook until eggs are desired consistency, stirring frequently.

4 Spoon egg mixture equally down center of warmed tortillas. Top equally with remaining cheese. Serve immediately. Refrigerate leftovers.

Serve with a side of fresh, sliced tomatoes or fresh fruit.

Variation: Use chopped Canadian bacon instead of ham. Use white flour tortillas.

Oven Omelet with Bacon, Chicken and Mushrooms

Preheat oven to 375°.

1 Butter an 8-inch-square baking pan.

2 Melt 2 tablespoons butter in a 10-inch nonstick skillet over medium heat. Add mushrooms. Cook, stirring occasionally until tender, about 4 minutes; drain.

3 Whisk milk, eggs, flour and black pepper in a medium bowl until frothy.

4 Stir in 1 cup cheese, bacon, chicken and mushrooms. Pour mixture into prepared baking pan. Sprinkle with remaining cheese. Bake until eggs are set in center, about 15 minutes.

Serve along with hot pancakes and maple syrup or buttered toast.

INGREDIENTS

2 tablespoons butter
2 cups sliced fresh mushrooms
$\frac{1}{3}$ cup whole milk
6 large eggs
2 tablespoons all-purpose flour
$\frac{1}{8}$ teaspoon ground black pepper
1 $\frac{1}{2}$ cups shredded Cheddar cheese, divided
6 slices crisply cooked bacon, crumbled
$\frac{1}{2}$ cup diced rotisserie chicken breast, skin removed

6 SERVINGS

Soups

Black-Eyed Pea Soup

1 Bring all ingredients except greens to a boil in a large soup pot. Reduce heat; cover and simmer 20 minutes.

2 Stir in greens until heated. Serve hot. Refrigerate leftovers.

Serve this southern soup with warm French bread.

When my husband, a true Norwegian, first heard about black-eyed peas, he was sure they were putting him on, but soon found out how delicious and nutritious they are.

INGREDIENTS

2 15-ounce cans seasoned black-eyed peas
1 32-ounce container vegetable or chicken stock
1 14-ounce can diced tomatoes with roasted garlic
1 cup chopped onion
½ cup chopped celery
½ cup sliced carrots
2 teaspoons Creole or Cajun seasoning, or to taste
½ cup diced rotisserie chicken, skin removed
½ cup diced fully cooked ham
1 cup fresh or canned mustard greens or spinach

6 SERVINGS

Chicken and Brown Rice Soup

INGREDIENTS

1 32-ounce package low-sodium
  chicken broth
1 14-ounce can diced tomatoes with
  basil, garlic and oregano
½ cup chopped onion
½ cup chopped celery
¼ cup chopped carrots
½ cup instant brown rice
⅛ teaspoon each dried herbs: basil,
  oregano, thyme, fennel and savory,
  or 1 teaspoon herbes de Provence
2½ cups diced rotisserie chicken,
  skin removed

4 SERVINGS

1 Bring first five ingredients to a boil in a medium, heavy saucepan.

2 Stir in rice and herbs. Reduce heat to medium. Cover and simmer about 15 minutes or until rice and vegetables are cooked. Add chicken; simmer 5 minutes. Serve hot. Refrigerate leftovers.

Serve with a tossed green salad and warm, crusty bread.

Chicken and Dumpling Soup

1 Bring the first nine ingredients to a boil in a large, heavy saucepan. Reduce heat; cover and simmer 10 minutes.

2 Stir in chicken gravy; bring mixture to a boil.

3 Stir baking mix and water in a bowl to form dough. Drop dough by ½-teaspoonfuls into hot soup. Cover and cook 10 minutes. Serve hot. Refrigerate leftovers.

A quick, creamy soup using purchased chicken gravy for the base.

INGREDIENTS

1 cup chopped yellow onion
1 cup chopped celery
1 cup chopped carrots
3 cups shredded rotisserie chicken, skin removed
1 49-ounce can reduced sodium chicken broth
¼ teaspoon oregano
¼ teaspoon thyme
¼ teaspoon ground black pepper
Salt, to taste
2 12-ounce jars chicken gravy
⅔ cup all-purpose baking mix, such as Bisquick®
6 tablespoons cold water

6 SERVINGS

Chicken Mac and Cheese Soup

INGREDIENTS

1 32-ounce container chicken stock
¾ cup uncooked elbow macaroni
1 tablespoon butter
½ cup minced yellow onion
½ cup minced celery
1 10-ounce container light
  Alfredo sauce
1¾ cups shredded sharp Cheddar
  cheese
1 cup diced rotisserie chicken breast,
  skin removed
Flat leaf parsley

6 SERVINGS

1 Bring chicken stock and macaroni to a boil in a large saucepan over high heat. Reduce heat to medium and cook 10 minutes, stirring occasionally.

2 Melt butter in a medium-sized skillet. Add onion and celery; cook and stir 5 minutes.

3 Stir in Alfredo sauce and Cheddar cheese; cook, stirring constantly, until cheese is melted. Add mixture and diced chicken to macaroni mixture. Simmer uncovered 5 minutes. Serve hot. Garnish with fresh parsley. Refrigerate leftovers.

Serve with side of green salad and crusty bread for a quick lunch or light supper.

Chicken Noodle Soup

1 Bring the first seven ingredients to a boil in a 3-quart saucepan over medium-high heat. Reduce heat, cover and simmer 5 minutes.

2 Stir in noodles. Cover and simmer until noodles are tender but firm and vegetables are just tender, about 10 minutes.

3 Stir in chicken and parsley; cook until thoroughly heated. Serve hot. Refrigerate leftovers.

Serve this quick-to-prepare homemade soup with cheesy breadsticks.

INGREDIENTS

4½ cups chicken broth
1 cup chopped onion
1 cup sliced carrots
1 cup sliced celery
1 teaspoon dried basil, crushed
1 teaspoon dried oregano, crushed
¼ teaspoon ground black pepper
1½ cups dry medium egg noodles
2 cups chopped rotisserie chicken, skin removed
4 tablespoons chopped flat leaf parsley

6 SERVINGS

Chicken Tortellini Soup

INGREDIENTS

8 cups chicken broth
1 14-ounce can stewed tomatoes
1 10-ounce package frozen chopped
  spinach, thawed
¼ cup grated Parmesan cheese
½ teaspoon salt
¼ teaspoon ground black pepper
1 9-ounce package refrigerated
  cheese tortellini
3 cups cubed rotisserie chicken,
  skin removed

6 SERVINGS

1 Bring chicken broth, tomatoes, spinach, cheese, salt and black pepper to a slow boil in a large soup pot. Reduce heat; cover and cook 10 minutes over medium heat.

2 Add tortellini and chicken; cook until tortellini is tender, about 8 minutes. Serve hot. Refrigerate leftovers.

Serve this delicious soup along with a mixed green salad and Italian breadsticks.

Czech Cabbage Ham Chicken Soup with Split Dumplings

1 Boil cabbage in a large pot for 10 minutes. Drain and finely chop; set aside.

2 Melt butter in a large saucepan over medium heat. Add onions; cook and stir until soft. Gradually add flour, stirring constantly, until well browned.

3 Pour chicken stock in all at once, whisking constantly.

4 Add reserved mushroom liquid; bring to a boil. Reduce heat to simmer. Add chopped mushrooms, chopped cabbage, salt and pepper, ham and chicken. Simmer a few minutes or to a desired consistency. Serve hot with split dumplings. Refrigerate leftovers.

Split Dumplings

1 Combine egg, milk, flour, baking powder and salt in a mixing bowl until smooth. Add bread cubes; mix well. Make 2 small balls from dough. Bring a large pot of water to a boil. Drop dough balls into boiling water; cook 10 minutes. Roll balls over and cook an additional 10 minutes. Remove immediately from water and cut in half to release steam. Serve; refrigerate leftovers.

Serve this hearty soup as a special meal for close friends.

INGREDIENTS

Half a head of green cabbage
½ cup butter
1 cup chopped yellow onions
⅓ cup all-purpose flour
5 cups chicken stock
½ cup dried morel mushrooms, soaked in 1 cup hot water, then drained and chopped (reserve liquid)
Salt and black pepper to taste
2 cups fully cooked smoked ham
1½ cups cubed rotisserie chicken

Split Dumplings
1 egg, beaten
½ cup milk
1 cup all-purpose flour
⅛ teaspoon baking powder
1 teaspoon salt
5 slices white bread, cubed

4 SERVINGS

Egg Drop Soup with Chicken and Noodles

INGREDIENTS

4 cups low-sodium chicken broth
1½ cups water
3 tablespoons low-sodium soy sauce
3 cloves garlic, smashed
1½ teaspoons ground ginger
4 ounces wide rice noodles or
  Pad Thai noodles, broken into
  3-inch-long pieces
2 tablespoons cornstarch
2 tablespoons cold water
2 eggs, lightly beaten in a small bowl
1½ cups shredded rotisserie chicken,
  skin removed
3 green onions, thinly sliced

6 SERVINGS

1 Bring broth, water, soy sauce, garlic and ginger to a boil over medium-high heat in a medium-sized saucepan, then reduce heat to medium and cook for 10 minutes. Remove smashed garlic cloves; discard.

2 Add noodles to mixture; cook until tender, about 4 minutes.

3 Mix cornstarch and water in a small bowl; whisk mixture into broth and cook until thickened, about 1 minute.

4 Stir soup so it is moving in a circular direction. Pour beaten eggs in a slow steady stream. Stir in chicken. Serve hot and top with green onions. Refrigerate leftovers.

This Asian-style soup is so easy to prepare.

Green Pozole

1 Add stock, salsa and hominy to a large stockpot. Simmer over medium heat for 15 minutes.

2 Add chicken; simmer 5 minutes or until heated through. Serve. Refrigerate leftovers.

Ladle this Mexican soup into individual bowls. The soup is traditionally served with assorted bowls of diced avocado, shredded raw cabbage, diced onion, diced radish, crushed red pepper and Mexican oregano, allowing each person to choose the topping preferred. Serve with warmed tortillas.

INGREDIENTS

1 32-ounce carton chicken stock
1 16-ounce jar salsa verde (medium)
1 15-ounce can white hominy, drained
2 cups shredded rotisserie chicken, skin removed

4 SERVINGS

Hearty Chicken Vegetable Soup

INGREDIENTS

1 cup uncooked elbow macaroni
3 14-ounce cans chicken broth
½ cup chopped yellow onions
1 cup chopped rotisserie chicken,
  skin removed
1 15-ounce can pinto beans, drained
1 12-ounce package frozen
  vegetables containing broccoli,
  cauliflower and carrots
2 teaspoons dried basil leaves
½ teaspoon dried thyme leaves
Salt and black pepper to taste

6 SERVINGS

1 Cook macaroni according to package directions; drain.

2 Bring chicken broth and onions to a slow boil in a 4-quart saucepan over medium-high heat; cook 6 minutes, stirring occasionally.

3 Stir in chicken, beans, frozen vegetables, basil and thyme. Cook, stirring occasionally, until vegetables are cooked, about 6 minutes. Season with salt and pepper as desired.

4 Stir in cooked macaroni; cook until heated thoroughly. Serve hot. Refrigerate leftovers.

Top each serving with shredded Monterey Jack cheese for extra goodness.

Hot and Sour Chicken Soup

1 Combine soup mix and water in a medium saucepan. Bring mixture to a boil over medium heat, stirring frequently. Reduce heat; simmer 5 minutes.

2 Stir in remaining ingredients; cook 5 minutes. Serve. Refrigerate leftovers.

A packaged soup mix is used for this speedy soup.

INGREDIENTS

1 1.34-ounce package hot and sour soup mix
3 cups water
1 cup diced rotisserie chicken, skin removed
8 ounces firm silken tofu, cut into thin strips
½ cup bamboo shoots cut into thin strips
¼ cup green onion tops, minced

3 SERVINGS

Kale and Lentil Chicken Soup

INGREDIENTS

1 tablespoon corn or vegetable oil
1 cup chopped yellow onions
1 cup coarsely chopped carrots
2 cloves garlic, minced
6 cups low-sodium chicken broth
4 cups coarsely chopped fresh kale
1 tablespoon snipped fresh basil or
   1 teaspoon dried basil, crushed
¼ teaspoon salt
⅛ teaspoon black pepper
1½ cups cubed rotisserie chicken,
   skin removed
1 medium tomato, seeded and
   chopped
1 cup dried red lentils

6 SERVINGS

1 Heat oil in a large nonstick saucepan over medium-low heat. Add onions, carrots and garlic; cover and cook, stirring occasionally, 5 minutes.

2 Add chicken broth, kale, basil, salt and black pepper. Cover and simmer 10 minutes.

3 Stir in chicken, tomato and lentils. Cover and simmer until kale and lentils are tender, about 5 minutes. Serve hot. Refrigerate leftovers.

Kale and lentils are the stars in this delicious quick-to-prepare soup.

Kids' Favorite Chicken Noodle Soup

1 Place all ingredients in a large soup pot; cook uncovered 15 minutes. Serve hot. Refrigerate leftovers.

Serve this lunch with multi-grain bread . . . and a chocolate chip cookie for dessert!

6 cups chicken broth
2 cups shredded rotisserie chicken, skin removed
1 cup uncooked fine egg noodles
1 teaspoon thyme
1 cup diced fresh or frozen vegetables

4 SERVINGS

Ruth's Chicken and Vegetable Soup

INGREDIENTS

2 tablespoons extra virgin olive oil
4 cloves garlic, chopped
1 teaspoon chopped fresh oregano (or
    ¼ teaspoon dried oregano)
1 cup frozen or fresh corn
Half of a red bell pepper, chopped
1 quart low-sodium chicken broth
¼ cup tomato sauce
2 cups shredded rotisserie chicken,
    skin removed
Salt and black pepper to taste
1 cup fresh or frozen thinly sliced okra
1 small zucchini, chopped
1 tablespoon minced yellow onion
1 cup cooked elbow macaroni
4 green onions, thinly sliced, optional
¼ cup fresh sliced basil, optional

6 SERVINGS

1 Heat olive oil in a large pot over medium-high heat. Add garlic and oregano; cook just until garlic begins to sizzle (do not brown). Stir in corn and bell pepper; cook and stir 3 minutes.

2 Stir in broth, tomato sauce, chicken, salt and pepper. Bring to a boil. Add okra, zucchini and minced onion. Reduce heat and simmer until okra is tender, about 5 minutes. Add cooked macaroni; cook until heated through.

3 Remove soup from heat. Stir in green onions and basil. Serve hot. Refrigerate leftovers.

My sister Ruth often adds sliced smoked sausage to this soup.

Serve with crisp crackers or warm, crusty bread.

Tortilla Chicken Soup

1 Heat olive oil in a large saucepan over medium-high heat. Add bell pepper, onion and jalapeño; cook and stir 5 minutes. Add chili powder; cook and stir 1 minute. Stir in chicken broth and water. Bring mixture to a boil, then reduce heat to medium and simmer for 10 minutes.

2 Stir in chicken, tomatoes, beans, lime juice and salt. Cook mixture until warmed through, about 4 minutes. Serve hot in soup bowls topped with avocado and tortilla chips as desired. Refrigerate leftovers.

*Do not touch your eyes when working with jalapeños!

A quick savory southwestern-style soup.

INGREDIENTS

1 tablespoon olive oil
1 medium green bell pepper, chopped
1 small yellow onion, chopped
1 jalapeño pepper, seeded and finely chopped, or to taste*
1 tablespoon chili powder
5 cups low-sodium chicken broth
1 cup cold water
3 cups shredded rotisserie chicken, skin removed
1 14-ounce can diced tomatoes
1 14-ounce can black beans, drained and rinsed
2 tablespoons lime juice
½ teaspoon salt
1 firm, ripe avocado, peeled, pitted and cut into chunks
1 cup crumbled baked tortilla chips

4 SERVINGS

Sandwiches & Pitas

Bacon and Chicken Ranch Subs

1 Layer bottom of each bun with chicken, 2 slices bacon and equal amounts of cheese.

2 Place on an ungreased baking sheet. Broil until cheese is melted, about 1 to 2 minutes.

3 Remove from oven. Top with ranch dressing and lettuce. Serve. Refrigerate leftovers.

Serve with fries or potato chips along with sliced fresh fruit.

Variation: Cook your own bacon.

INGREDIENTS

4 brat buns, sliced in half horizontally
2 cups warm, shredded rotisserie chicken, skin removed
8 strips pre-cooked bacon
½ cup shredded mozzarella cheese
⅓ cup ranch dressing
1 cup shredded lettuce

4 SERVINGS

Barbecue Chicken Buns

INGREDIENTS

½ cup cider vinegar
¼ cup brown sugar, packed
1 8-ounce can tomato sauce
1 6-ounce can tomato paste
1 small onion, thinly sliced
½ teaspoon liquid smoke
¼ teaspoon salt
¼ teaspoon black pepper
3 cups shredded rotisserie chicken,
  skin removed
6 onion buns, cut in half
1 medium green bell pepper, sliced
  into 12 rings
¾ cup shredded mozzarella cheese

6 SERVINGS

1 Mix first eight ingredients in a 2-quart saucepan. Cook over medium heat, stirring occasionally, until slightly thickened, about 10 minutes. Stir in shredded chicken; cook and stir until heated.

2 Place bottom half of buns on an ungreased baking sheet. Spoon barbecue mixture equally onto bun bottoms. Top equally with green pepper rings; sprinkle equally with cheese.

3 Broil 2 to 4 inches from heat until cheese is melted, about 2 minutes. Top with remaining bun halves. Serve. Refrigerate leftovers.

Serve this tangy sandwich with sweet corn on the cob.

 Variation: Use your favorite purchased barbecue sauce.

Cheddar, Chicken and Artichoke Melts

Preheat oven to 375°.

1 Stir first five ingredients in a medium bowl until well mixed.

2 Spread mixture equally and evenly over 4 toasted bread slices. Top with cheese. Place on a baking sheet; bake until hot and cheese is melted, about 6 minutes. Top with remaining toasted bread. Serve. Refrigerate leftovers.

Variation: Use rye bread.

INGREDIENTS

2 cups chopped rotisserie chicken, skin removed
1 6-ounce jar marinated artichoke hearts, drained and finely chopped
3 tablespoons mayonnaise
2 tablespoons finely chopped red onion
1 tablespoon Dijon or course mustard
8 slices sourdough bread, lightly toasted
8 slices sharp Cheddar cheese, cut in half diagonally

4 SERVINGS

Chicken Quesadillas

INGREDIENTS

1 large onion, halved lengthwise and
  thinly sliced crosswise
2 tablespoons vegetable oil
2 large fresh garlic cloves, thinly sliced
3½ cups shredded rotisserie chicken,
  skin removed
¾ teaspoons salt
½ teaspoon ground black pepper
2 cups (5 ounces) coarsely grated
  Monterey Jack cheese
8 (7-inch) flour tortillas

4 SERVINGS

1 Cook onion in oil in medium-sized nonstick skillet over medium heat until golden, about 6 minutes. Add garlic; cook and stir 1 minute. Place in a large bowl.

2 Add chicken, salt, black pepper and cheese to bowl; stir.

3 Put 1 tortilla on a cutting board and spread ½ cup of mixture over half of the tortilla, then fold other half over to form a half-moon, pressing firmly on seam. Continue with remaining tortillas and mixture.

4 Heat a lightly oiled grill pan over high heat until it begins to smoke. Reduce heat to medium and grill quesadillas, 2 at a time, turning over once, until cheese is melted and golden brown and grill marks appear, about 4 minutes total per batch. Transfer with a spatula to a cutting board and cut in half. Serve warm. Refrigerate leftovers.

Serve with sour cream and salsa along with a side of warm red beans and rice.

Chicken Bagel Melts

1 Split bagels and spread bottoms with mayonnaise.

2 Layer each bottom with chicken, bacon, bell pepper and cheese. Place on an ungreased baking sheet.

3 Broil 2 to 4 inches from heat about 2 to 3 minutes or until cheese is melted.

4 Remove from oven. Spread mustard over bagel tops and place over cheese. Serve immediately. Refrigerate leftovers.

This chicken sandwich is so easy to prepare. Serve with a side of fresh fruit.

Tip: Use ready-to-serve fully cooked bacon.

INGREDIENTS

4 cheese bagels
½ cup mayonnaise
2 cups thinly sliced rotisserie chicken breast, skin removed
8 strips cooked bacon, drained
½ medium red bell pepper, sliced
4 slices sharp Cheddar cheese
¼ cup chipotle mustard

4 SERVINGS

Chicken Caesar Sandwich

INGREDIENTS

1 1-pound loaf rustic bread, such as ciabatta
1 cup bottled Caesar salad dressing
2 boneless, skinless, rotisserie chicken breasts, sliced
3 cups bagged hearts of romaine lettuce
¼ cup shredded Parmesan cheese
Ground black pepper to taste

6 SERVINGS

1 Split bread in half lengthwise. Spread dressing over both cut sides.

2 Pile chicken on half of the loaf. Top with romaine and cheese. Season with black pepper to taste. Top with top half of bread.

3 Cut into 6 portions using a serrated knife. Serve. Refrigerate leftovers.

Caesar salad lovers will enjoy this sandwich.

Variation: Other breads may be used.

Chicken Club Sandwiches

Preheat oven to 400°.

1 Line a baking sheet with cooking foil.

2 Place bread on baking sheet. Top with chicken, tomato, bacon and cheese.

3 Bake until sandwiches are hot and cheese is melted, about 5 to 7 minutes. Serve immediately. Refrigerate leftovers.

Serve these open-faced sandwiches with a fruit salad and iced tea.

INGREDIENTS

4 1-inch-thick slices potato rosemary bread, lightly toasted
2 cups warm, shredded rotisserie chicken, skin removed
8 small slices fresh tomatoes
8 slices pre-cooked bacon
2 large slices Havarti cheese, halved

4 SERVINGS

Chicken Salad Sandwiches

INGREDIENTS

1 ½ cups chopped rotisserie chicken
    breast, skin removed
½ cup mayonnaise or salad dressing
½ cup chopped celery
¼ cup chopped yellow onion
¼ teaspoon salt, or to taste
¼ teaspoon ground black pepper
8 slices good quality white bread,
    buttered

4 SERVINGS

1 Mix all ingredients except bread in a bowl; adjust seasoning.

2 Spoon equal amounts of filling mixture onto 4 slices of bread. Top with remaining slices. Cut diagonally. Serve. Refrigerate leftovers.

Serve with potato chips and pickles.

Variations: Use whole wheat bread. Add lettuce.

Grilled Buffalo Blue Sandwiches

1 Mix chicken, celery and sauce in a medium bowl; set aside.

2 Cut bread into 16 ½-inch-thick slices. Butter one side of each slice.

3 Spread about 1 teaspoon salad dressing onto other side of each bread slice.

4 Place 1 piece cheese over dressing on 8 slices, then top with ⅓ cup chicken mixture, 1 piece cheese and remaining bread slices, butter-side up.

5 Place sandwiches onto grill. Grill turning once, until bread is toasted and cheese is melted. Serve. Refrigerate leftovers.

A flavorful sandwich to grill on gas or charcoal grill.

INGREDIENTS

2 cups shredded rotisserie chicken, skin removed
¾ cup chopped celery
¼ cup buffalo wing sauce
1 1-pound loaf French bread
¼ cup butter, softened
⅓ cup blue cheese salad dressing
8 slices deli provolone cheese, cut in half into 16 pieces

8 SERVINGS

Mexican Chicken Subs

INGREDIENTS

4 soft French (poor boy) rolls
4 slices pepper jack cheese, cut in half into 8 pieces
3 cups warm, shredded rotisserie chicken, skin removed
1 cup salsa
⅓ cup sliced green onions
1 2.2-ounce can sliced ripe olives, drained

4 SERVINGS

Preheat oven to 400°.

1 Cut a section out of the top of each roll and tear out some of the inside to make a bread bowl. Place 1 piece of cheese in the bottom of each roll.

2 Mix chicken, salsa, onions and olives in a medium bowl. Spoon into bread bowls and top each with remaining cheese.

3 Place on an ungreased baking sheet and tent loosely with aluminum foil. Cook until sandwiches are hot and cheese is melted, about 15 minutes. Serve. Refrigerate leftovers.

Serve with tortilla or corn chips along with frosty cold drinks.

Nelan's Muffuletta Sandwich

Olive Salad

1 Mix all salad ingredients in a medium-sized glass bowl and refrigerate for 2 hours.

Sandwich

1 Spread half of the olive salad on bottom half of partially hollowed out bread. Layer with meats and cheeses, then top with remaining olive salad.

2 Cover with the top of bread; press down and let stand 5 minutes. Cut into 6 wedges using a serrated knife. Wrap wedges in plastic wrap until serving. Refrigerate leftovers.

The "Big Easy" sandwich is a winner in New Orleans and Eunice, Louisiana!

INGREDIENTS

Olive Salad
1 cup pitted green olives, coarsely chopped
1 cup pitted black olives, coarsely chopped
⅓ cup diced, roasted red bell pepper
¼ cup diced celery with leaves
2 tablespoons chopped flat leaf parsley
2 teaspoons finely minced garlic
2 tablespoons red wine vinegar
2 tablespoons olive oil
Salt and ground black pepper to taste

Sandwich
1 round Italian or peasant bread (about 7 inches in diameter and 5 inches high), split crosswise and most of insides pulled out and discarded.
2 ounces thinly sliced mortadella (found in deli section)
2 ounces thinly sliced fully cooked ham
2 ounces thinly sliced garlic-flavored rotisserie chicken breast, skin removed
2 ounces thinly sliced Genoa salami
2 ounces sliced mozzarella cheese
2 ounces sliced provolone cheese

6 SERVINGS

Pesto Chicken Panini

INGREDIENTS

½ cup shredded rotisserie chicken,
  skin removed
1 tablespoon pesto
2 slices multi-grain bread
¼ cup shredded part-skim
  mozzarella cheese

1 SERVING

Preheat panini grill to high.

1 Mix chicken and pesto in a bowl; spread mixture onto 1 bread slice. Top with cheese and remaining bread slice.

2 Grill about 3 to 5 minutes, or until cheese is melted and sandwich is golden brown on both sides. Serve. Refrigerate leftovers.

This is a good recipe for one person. Serve with a side of chips and fruit.

Tip: If you don't have a panini grill, preheat a large heavy skillet on medium heat. Cook sandwich on both sides, pressing down top with a spatula to flatten.

Sloppy Joes

1 Heat corn oil in a 10-inch nonstick skillet. Add onions, celery and bell pepper; cook and stir 5 minutes.

2 Stir in remaining ingredients except hamburger buns; cover and cook over low heat just until vegetables are tender, about 10 minutes.

3 Fill buns with mixture. Serve hot. Refrigerate leftovers.

Always a favorite with kids…and grown-ups too! Serve with potato chips and a favorite cola or lemonade.

INGREDIENTS

1 tablespoon corn oil
1 medium yellow onion, chopped
⅓ cup chopped celery
⅓ cup chopped green bell pepper
⅓ cup ketchup
¼ cup water
1 tablespoon Worcestershire sauce
1 teaspoon salt
⅛ teaspoon hot pepper sauce
3 cups chopped rotisserie chicken, skin removed
6 hamburger buns, buttered

6 SERVINGS

Vietnamese Chicken Sandwiches

INGREDIENTS

2½ cups shredded coleslaw blend
    (green and purple cabbage
    and carrots)
1½ cups shredded rotisserie chicken,
    skin removed
⅓ cup Asian salad dressing
¼ cup sliced green onions
⅛ teaspoon Chinese five spice powder
1 baguette, halved lengthwise

4 SERVINGS

1 Mix all ingredients except baguette in a medium bowl.

2 Spoon mixture evenly onto baguette bottom; top with baguette top. Cut into 4 equal pieces. Serve. Refrigerate leftovers.

Serve this delicious sandwich with a side of fresh cantaloupe.

Cheddar Apple Chicken Pitas

1 Mix chicken, apple, celery, mayonnaise and mustard in a medium bowl.

2 Cut pitas into halves; open each pita half and line with a piece of cheese and one lettuce leaf. Fill each pocket equally with chicken mixture. Serve. Refrigerate leftovers.

Serve with a fresh fruit salad.

 Variations: Use white pita bread. Use Colby cheese.

INGREDIENTS

2 cups chopped rotisserie chicken, skin removed
½ cup diced unpeeled apple
½ cup diced celery
¼ cup light mayonnaise
1 tablespoon Dijon or spicy brown mustard
4 (6-inch) whole wheat pita breads
4 slices deli-style sliced Cheddar cheese, cut in half into 8 pieces
8 romaine lettuce leaves

4 SERVINGS

Cobb Salad Chicken Pitas

INGREDIENTS

1 cup diced rotisserie chicken,
  skin removed
⅛ teaspoon black pepper
1 cup shredded Cheddar Jack cheese
1 cup chopped fresh ripe tomato
1 ripe avocado, peeled, pitted
  and diced
⅓ cup crisply cooked bacon, crumbled
  (or real bacon bits)
⅓ cup Thousand Island or Italian
  salad dressing
4 (6-inch) pita breads, halved
romaine lettuce or red leaf lettuce

4 SERVINGS

1 Mix all ingredients except pita bread and lettuce in a
  medium bowl.

2 Open pita halves; line each with lettuce leaves and fill equally
  with chicken mixture. Serve. Refrigerate leftovers.

Serve with fresh melon wedges and grapes.

Fresh Slaw and Chicken Pita

1 Heat 1 tablespoon salad dressing in a large nonstick skillet. Add chicken and chili pepper; cook and stir over medium-high heat 3 minutes. Remove chicken mixture to a large bowl.

2 Add 3 tablespoons salad dressing to the same skillet. Stir in 1 cup of slaw at a time, adding more as slaw begins to wilt. Season with salt and pepper. Cook until all slaw is wilted.

3 Stir slaw mixture into chicken mixture in bowl. Fill pita bread pockets equally with mixture. Refrigerate leftovers.

Serve with a fresh fruit salad.

INGREDIENTS

4 tablespoons vinegar and oil salad dressing, divided
3 cups rotisserie chicken breast strips
1 mild chili pepper, seeded and coarsely chopped, optional
1 pound package ready-to-use cabbage slaw
¼ teaspoon salt
¼ teaspoon ground black pepper
4 white or whole wheat pita bread pockets

4 SERVINGS

Tacos & Wraps

Chicken and Rice Soft Tacos

1 Heat corn oil in a large skillet over medium-high heat. Add chicken; cook and stir 2 minutes.

2 Add water, salsa and taco seasoning. Bring to a boil. Stir in rice. Cover and cook over low heat for 6 minutes. Remove from heat and let stand a few minutes.

3 Spoon mixture onto warm tortillas. Sprinkle with cheese. Fold sides up and serve immediately. Refrigerate leftovers.

Serve with canned, hot chili beans and a favorite beverage.

INGREDIENTS

1 tablespoon corn oil
2½ cups thin strips of rotisserie chicken breast, skin removed, seasoned with ⅛ teaspoon black pepper
2 cups water
1 cup purchased thick and chunky mild salsa
1 1.25-ounce package taco seasoning
2 cups instant rice, uncooked
10 (6-inch) flour tortillas, warmed
¼ cup reduced fat shredded Cheddar cheese

5 SERVINGS

Chicken Soft Tacos

INGREDIENTS

1 rotisserie chicken, bones and skin
   removed
2 7-ounce cans salsa verde
1½ teaspoons Mexican seasoning
12 corn tortillas, warmed
1 15-ounce can ranch-style black
   beans, warmed
1 cup shredded Mexican-blend cheese

Toppings
Shredded iceberg lettuce
Diced tomatoes
Green onions
Sour cream
Guacamole

6 SERVINGS

1 Tear chicken into bite-sized pieces. Combine with salsa verde and seasoning in a skillet. Cook over medium heat until warmed, about 5 minutes.

2 Spoon mixture equally onto heated tortillas. Top with black beans and cheese. Serve with toppings as desired.

Black beans and Mexican cheese fill these soft tacos.

Variations: Use flour tortillas.

Simple Chicken Tacos

1 Pull chicken into long shreds. Heat salsa in a large saucepan. Stir in chicken; heat over medium heat until warmed.

2 Fill taco shells with mixture; top with cheese and green onion.

3 Serve with sour cream and avocado on the side.

Serve these tacos along with a lettuce and tomato salad.

Variation: Use soft corn or flour tortillas instead of taco shells.

INGREDIENTS

1 rotisserie chicken, bones and skin removed
2 cups purchased red or green salsa
8 taco shells
1 cup grated Cheddar cheese
¼ cup finely sliced green onion
½ cup sour cream
1 avocado, peeled, pitted and chopped

4 SERVINGS

Bacon Lettuce Tomato Chicken Wraps

INGREDIENTS

2 medium fresh tomatoes, seeded
  and chopped
1 cup (4 ounces) finely shredded
  Cheddar cheese
⅓ cup ranch salad dressing
4 large (10-inch) flour tortillas
2 cups shredded iceberg lettuce
12 slices bacon, crisply cooked
  and crumbled
1 cup shredded rotisserie chicken
  breast, skin removed

4 WRAPS

1 Mix tomatoes, cheese and salad dressing in a medium bowl.

2 Warm tortillas and place individually on parchment paper.

3 Place ½ cup lettuce in the center of one tortilla. Top with one-quarter each of tomato mixture, bacon and chicken. Fold in about 1 inch on sides of tortilla and roll up, starting at bottom edge, to encase filling. Repeat with remaining ingredients. Serve warm or chilled. Refrigerate leftovers.

Kids love these wraps. Serve with a favorite beverage.

Variation: Add thinly sliced green onions.

Tip: To re-warm wraps, leave wraps in parchment paper; microwave on high for 30 seconds per wrap or until warmed. Serve immediately. Refrigerate leftovers.

Barbecue Chicken Coleslaw Wrap

1 Heat chicken and barbecue sauce in a small saucepan; set aside.

2 Warm tortillas on paper towel in microwave on high power for 10 seconds.

3 Layer each tortilla with a lettuce leaf. Spread ½ cup chicken mixture and ¼ cup coleslaw across the middle of tortilla. Top with 2 cheese halves.

4 Bring edges of tortilla over filling; secure with toothpick. Serve. Refrigerate leftovers.

Serve this tangy, crunchy wrap along with corn on the cob.

Tip: When serving, wrap the filled tortillas in waxed paper to avoid drips.

INGREDIENTS

2 cups chopped rotisserie chicken, skin removed
½ cup barbecue sauce
4 (10-inch) flour tortillas
4 lettuce leaves
1 cup prepared deli coleslaw, drained
4 sliced deli American cheese, cut in half diagonally into 8 pieces

4 SERVINGS

Caesar Chicken Wraps

INGREDIENTS

2 cups chopped rotisserie chicken,
   skin removed
4 slices bacon, cooked and crumbled
3 cups shredded romaine lettuce
¼ cup shredded Parmesan cheese
¼ cup croutons, purchased or
   homemade
½ cup Caesar salad dressing
4 (8-inch) flour tortillas, warmed

4 SERVINGS

1 Toss all ingredients except tortillas in a large bowl until coated.

2 Spoon equal amounts of mixture across the middle of each tortilla; roll up tightly. Serve. Refrigerate leftovers.

Serve with fresh fruit.

 Variation: Use ranch salad dressing.

Chicken Rice Wraps

1 Stir and cook rice-vermicelli mix with margarine in a large nonstick skillet over medium-high heat until vermicelli is golden brown.

2 Slowly stir in water, tomatoes and seasonings in rice-vermicelli packet; bring mixture to a boil. Reduce heat to low. Cover and simmer 15 minutes.

3 Stir in chicken; cook, covered, 5 minutes or until rice is tender.

4 Stir in beans and corn; let stand 5 minutes before serving. Serve in warm tortillas with cheese and sour cream as desired. Refrigerate leftovers.

A packaged rice mix makes it so easy to prepare these delicious wraps. Serve along with a crisp green salad or sliced fresh cantaloupe.

Variation: Use 1 (16-ounce) jar purchased salsa instead of tomatoes.

INGREDIENTS

1 6.8-ounce package Spanish rice-vermicelli mix, such as Rice-A-Roni®
2 tablespoons margarine or butter
2 cups cold water
2 cups chopped fresh tomatoes
3 cups thin strips of rotisserie chicken breast, skin removed
1 cup canned black beans or canned kidney beans, drained and rinsed
1 cup frozen or canned corn, drained
8 (6-inch) flour tortillas, warmed
Shredded Cheddar cheese
Sour cream

4 SERVINGS

Egg with Bacon and Chicken Luncheon Wrap

INGREDIENTS

1 ½ tablespoons butter
1 medium yellow onion, chopped
¾ cup chopped green bell pepper
5 eggs
1 tablespoon whole milk
½ teaspoon salt
¼ teaspoon ground black pepper
2 cups shredded Cheddar cheese
8 slices bacon, crisply cooked and
  crumbled
1 cup diced rotisserie chicken breast,
  skin removed
4 (10-inch) flour tortillas, warmed

4 SERVINGS

1 Heat butter in a large nonstick skillet. Cook and stir onion and bell pepper until tender.

2 Beat eggs, milk, salt and pepper in a medium bowl. Pour mixture over cooked vegetables in skillet.

3 Sprinkle with cheese, bacon and chicken. Cook and stir gently over medium heat until eggs are completely set.

4 Spoon ½ cup mixture down the center of each tortilla; fold sides over filling. Serve. Refrigerate leftovers.

Serve these luncheon wraps with salsa and a side of cantaloupe.

Variation: Serve for breakfast.

Mu Shu-Style Chicken Wraps

1 Heat dressing in a large skillet over medium heat. Stir in coleslaw blend, chicken and cashews until coated. Bring mixture to a boil, stirring frequently. Remove from heat. Stir in parsley.

2 Spoon about ½ cup of mixture down the center of each tortilla; roll up. Serve immediately.

Serve with fresh melon wedges and assorted fresh fruit.

INGREDIENTS

¾ cup Asian sesame with ginger dressing
3½ cups bagged coleslaw blend
2 cups finely chopped rotisserie chicken, skin removed
½ cup cashew pieces
1 tablespoon chopped fresh parsley or cilantro
8 (8-inch) flour tortillas, warmed

8 SERVINGS

Muffuletta Wraps

INGREDIENTS

½ cup chopped pimento-stuffed olives
½ cup chopped pitted Kalamata or
  black olives
½ cup giardinera vegetables (pickled
  vegetables), drained and chopped
¼ cup chopped fresh parsley
2 tablespoon olive oil
¼ teaspoon ground black pepper
4 (10-inch) flour tortillas
4 lettuce leaves
8 slices hard salami
8 slices Provolone cheese
8 thin slices rotisserie chicken breast,
  skin removed

4 SERVINGS

1 Mix olives, pickled vegetables, parsley, olive oil and black pepper in a small bowl.

2 Line each tortilla with a lettuce leaf, 2 slices salami, 2 slices cheese and 2 slices chicken. Top each with a heaping ¼ cup olive mixture. Fold ends in and roll up tortilla. Wrap each in plastic food wrap and refrigerate until serving time. Refrigerate leftovers.

These muffuletta wraps are akin to the muffuletta sandwiches popular in New Orleans.

Variations: Use flavored tortillas. Add a thin slice of fully cooked ham.

Tex-Mex Chicken and Cheese Wraps

1 Stir together the first seven ingredients in a large bowl. Spoon about 1 cup of filling in the center of each warmed tortilla. Fold two opposite sides of tortilla toward center, over filling. Roll up open end of tortilla toward opposite edge.

2 Place two filled tortillas at a time on a microwave-safe plate, seam side down.

3 Microwave 2 tortillas on medium-high power, until heated through, about 1 to 2 minutes, turning or rearranging after half the time. Repeat with remaining tortillas. Serve immediately. Refrigerate leftovers.

This is a delicious meal wrapped in a tortilla. Serve with salsa.

 Tip: Cut tortillas in half when serving for easier handling.

INGREDIENTS

1 cup cooked rice
¾ cup salsa, purchased or homemade
3 thinly sliced green onions
1 15-ounce can black beans, rinsed
  and drained
1 11-ounce can whole kernel corn
  with red and green peppers, drained
1 cup cubed ½-inch rotisserie chicken,
  skin removed
1 8-ounce package Cheddar cheese,
  cut into ½-inch cubes
6 (10-inch) flour tortillas, warmed

6 SERVINGS

Pizza

Barbecue Mango Chicken Pizza

Preheat oven to 450°.

1 Spread 2 tablespoons barbecue sauce on each pizza crust; sprinkle each with ½ cup cheese. Top with equal amounts of mango, chicken, bacon bits and green onions.

2 Bake about 10 to 12 minutes, rotating pizzas occasionally for even cooking (cheese should be melted and lightly browned around the edges).

To make 6 small servings, cut each pizza in half.

INGREDIENTS

6 tablespoons barbecue sauce
1 12-ounce package 7-inch pizza crusts
1½ cups shredded Italian blend cheese
1½ cups bite-sized pieces fresh mango
1 cup shredded rotisserie chicken, skin removed
¼ cup real bacon bits
¼ cup sliced green onion

3 LARGE SERVINGS

BBQ Chicken Chicago-Style Pizza Bagels

INGREDIENTS

4 whole wheat bagels, cut in half
2 cups shredded rotisserie chicken, skin removed
½ cup BBQ sauce (your favorite)
3 tablespoons chopped red onions
½ cup chopped fresh cilantro
1½ cups shredded part-skim mozzarella cheese
1 cup canned Italian-style diced tomatoes

8 SERVINGS

Preheat oven to 400°.

1 Line a baking sheet with aluminum foil. Place bagel halves on the lined sheet.

2 Mix chicken, barbecue sauce, red onions and cilantro in a medium bowl. Top each bagel half with ¼ cup chicken mixture.

3 Sprinkle 3 tablespoons cheese over each half. Spoon ⅛ cup diced canned tomatoes on top of each bagel half.

4 Bake until cheese is melted and bagel is hot, about 10 to 12 minutes. Serve. Refrigerate leftovers.

Bagels are not just for cream cheese anymore!

Tip: Cut each bagel half into two pieces or serve as is.

Chicken and Spinach Pita Pizza

Preheat oven to 400°.

1 Heat olive oil in a small skillet over medium heat. Add onion; cook and stir 1 minute. Add spinach and oregano; cook and stir 1 minute or until spinach is wilted.

2 Sprinkle ¼ cup cheese on pitas. Top with spinach mixture, tomatoes and chicken. Sprinkle evenly with remaining cheese.

3 Place pitas on a baking sheet. Bake until cheese is melted, about 10 minutes. Serve. Refrigerate leftovers.

This is a quick and delicious pizza. Serve with fresh fruit.

Variation: Add sliced black olives.

INGREDIENTS

½ teaspoon olive oil
¼ cup thinly sliced red onion
3 cups chopped fresh spinach
¼ teaspoon dried oregano
1 cup shredded reduced fat
   mozzarella cheese, divided
2 (6-inch) pita breads
2 plum tomatoes, sliced
1 cup cubed rotisserie chicken breast,
   skin removed

2 SERVINGS

Chicken Ranch Pizza

INGREDIENTS

2 cups bite-sized rotisserie chicken, skin removed
⅔ cup ranch dressing, divided
1 12-inch prepared pizza crust
6 slices bacon, crisply cooked and crumbled
¼ cup sliced green onion
2 cups shredded mozzarella cheese
1 cup shredded Cheddar cheese

4 SERVINGS

Preheat oven to 400°.

1 Mix chicken and ⅓ cup ranch dressing in a medium bowl. Spread remaining ⅓ cup dressing over pizza crust. Spread chicken mixture over crust.

2 Top with bacon, onion and cheese. Bake until crust is browned and cheese is melted, about 14 minutes. Cut into wedges and serve. Refrigerate leftovers

Rotisserie chicken makes this pizza so easy to prepare.

Chicken and Spinach Tortilla Pizza

Preheat oven to 425°.

1 Line 2 baking sheets with aluminum foil. Place tortillas on baking sheets. Top each with equal amounts of all ingredients listed, in order given.

2 Bake about 8 to 10 minutes or until tortilla edges are lightly browned. Cut into wedges and serve. Refrigerate leftovers.

Flour tortillas are used for the pizza crusts.

 Variation: Add sautéed sliced mushrooms.

INGREDIENTS

4 soft taco-sized flour tortillas
½ cup purchased light Alfredo sauce
1 8-ounce package Italian cheese crumbles
1⅓ cups diced rotisserie chicken, skin removed
1 cup coarsely chopped fresh spinach
¼ cup sliced green onions
¼ cup chopped sun-dried tomatoes

4 SERVINGS

Chicken Pesto Pizza

INGREDIENTS

1 3.5-ounce jar prepared basil pesto
1 10-ounce can refrigerated pizza
  crust dough
4 small plum tomatoes, thinly sliced
1½ cups chopped rotisserie chicken,
  skin removed
¼ teaspoon ground black pepper
8 slices mozzarella cheese

6 SERVINGS

Preheat oven to 450°.

1 Spray 12-inch pizza pan with nonstick cooking spray. Unroll crust and press onto prepared pizza pan.

2 Spread pesto evenly over pizza crust. Top with tomatoes and chicken. Sprinkle with black pepper and top with cheese.

3 Bake about 10 minutes or until lightly browned. Cut into wedges. Serve. Refrigerate leftovers.

Serve with a green salad.

English Muffin Pizza

Preheat oven to 425°.

1 Lightly butter English muffin halves.

2 Spread each equally with pizza sauce. Sprinkle equally with cheese over sauce. Top each with 1 slice of chicken, then with pepperoni, divided equally.

3 Place on a baking sheet. Bake until cheese melts, about 5 minutes. Serve immediately. Refrigerate leftovers.

Serve along with a green salad for a light lunch.

INGREDIENTS

6 English muffin halves
¾ cup purchased pizza sauce
1½ cups shredded mozzarella cheese
6 thin slices rotisserie chicken breast, skin removed
3 ounces sliced pepperoni

6 SERVINGS

French Bread Pizza

INGREDIENTS

1 4-ounce French roll, cut in half
¼ cup pizza sauce
¼ cup cooked, crumbled Italian
   sausage
¼ cup finely diced rotisserie chicken
   breast, skin removed
½ cup shredded mozzarella-Cheddar
   cheese blend, or cheese of your
   choice
¼ cup black olives
¼ cup sliced green pepper strips
¼ cup thinly sliced onions
¼ cup sliced mushrooms

2 SERVINGS

Preheat oven to 350°.

1 Lightly toast both French roll halves.

2 Place on a baking sheet cut-side up. Spread with pizza sauce. Top with sausage, chicken and cheese. Add any of the remaining ingredients as desired.

3 Bake until cheese is melted, about 10 minutes. Serve. Refrigerate leftovers.

This is a quick, tasty pizza.

Variation: Use an Italian roll.

Fresh Vegetable Chicken Pizza

Preheat oven to 425°.

1 Spray 12-inch pizza pan with nonstick cooking spray. Unroll crust and press onto prepared pizza pan.

2 Heat corn oil in a medium-sized nonstick skillet. Add onions and garlic; stir and cook over medium heat for 2 minutes. Add bell pepper and mushrooms; stir and cook 2 minutes. Add diced chicken; stir and cook 1 minute. Remove skillet from heat; set aside.

3 Sprinkle ¾ cup cheese over crust. Arrange tomato slices over cheese; sprinkle with basil and oregano. Top with chicken mixture. Sprinkle with remaining cheese.

4 Bake until crust is crisp and cheese is melted, about 10 minutes.

Serve this simple pizza with a side of fresh watermelon wedges.

INGREDIENTS

1 (10-ounce) can refrigerated
  pizza crust
1 tablespoon corn oil
½ cup finely sliced red onions
2 cloves garlic, chopped
1 small green or red bell pepper cut
  into 1-inch strips
½ cup sliced fresh mushrooms
2 cups diced rotisserie chicken,
  skin removed
1½ cups light mozzarella shredded
  cheese, divided
4 plum tomatoes, sliced
1 teaspoon dried basil
½ teaspoon dried oregano

6 SERVINGS

Shrimp and Chicken Pesto Pizza

INGREDIENTS

1 12-inch prepared pizza crust
⅓ cup prepared pesto sauce
2 cups (8 ounces) shredded Italian
  6-cheese blend, divided
8 ounces cooked shrimp, shelled and
  deveined
1 cup diced rotisserie chicken breast,
  skin removed
½ cup coarsely chopped, softened
  sun-dried tomatoes
¼ cup minced green onions
¼ teaspoon crushed red pepper flakes,
  or to taste

6 SERVINGS

Preheat oven to 450°.

1 Place crust on a baking sheet. Spread evenly with pesto sauce.

2 Sprinkle with 1 cup cheese. Top with shrimp, chicken and tomatoes. Top with remaining cheese and sprinkle with onions and pepper flakes.

3 Bake until cheese is melted, about 10 minutes. Refrigerate leftovers.

Serve this tasty pizza along with a green salad.

Variations: Use a 16-ounce Italian bread shell. Use 4 sliced plum (Roma) tomatoes instead of sun-dried tomatoes.

Stuffed Crust Pepperoni and Chicken Pizza

Preheat oven to 425°.

1 Grease a 13x9-inch baking pan. Unroll crust. Press onto bottom and 1 inch up the sides of prepared baking pan.

2 Place pieces of string cheese along inside edges of crust. Fold sides of crust over and around cheese; press crust edges to seal.

3 Top with pizza sauce, pepperoni, chicken and cheese.

4 Bake until crust is golden and cheese is melted, about 15 minutes. Refrigerate leftovers.

Cheese lovers, this one's for you.

INGREDIENTS

1 10-ounce can refrigerated
   pizza crust
6 pieces string cheese
½ cup pizza sauce
20 slices pepperoni
1 cup thinly sliced rotisserie chicken
   breast strips, skin removed
1 cup shredded Italian 6-cheese blend

6 SERVINGS

Three-Meat Crescent Pizza

INGREDIENTS

1 8-ounce can refrigerated crescent
dinner rolls
1 12-ounce package bulk sausage
1 cup shredded rotisserie chicken
breast, skin removed
4 slices crisply cooked bacon,
crumbled
1 cup frozen shredded hash
brown potatoes
½ cup Cheddar cheese
4 eggs
½ teaspoon salt
⅛ teaspoon ground black pepper
3 tablespoons milk

6 SERVINGS

Preheat oven to 375°.

1 Unroll crescent rolls; separate into 4 rectangles. Place in an ungreased 13x9-inch baking pan. Press over bottom and ½ inch up sides to form crust; firmly press perforations and edges to seal.

2 Crumble and cook sausage in an 8-inch nonstick skillet over medium-high heat, stirring frequently, until cooked and no longer pink; drain. Spoon cooked sausage evenly over crust. Sprinkle with chicken, bacon, potatoes and cheese.

3 Beat eggs in a medium bowl with salt, pepper and milk; pour mixture over cheese in crust.

4 Bake until center is set and edges are deep golden brown, about 18 to 20 minutes. Cut into serving pieces. Serve. Refrigerate leftovers.

Serve this pizza for breakfast or lunch with salsa and a favorite beverage.

White Chicken Pizza

Preheat oven to 450°.

1 Melt butter in a 1-quart saucepan over low heat. Add garlic; cook and stir 2 minutes.

2 Place pizza crust onto a large ungreased baking sheet. Spread garlic-butter mixture evenly over crust.

3 Sprinkle with ¾ cup cheese. Sprinkle chicken and parsley evenly over crust. Top evenly with remaining cheese.

4 Bake until cheese is melted and lightly browned, about 9 to 11 minutes. Cut into wedges. Serve. Refrigerate leftovers.

This flavorful pizza is ready to go in minutes.

INGREDIENTS

2 tablespoons butter
1 teaspoon finely chopped fresh garlic
1 14-ounce round, pre-baked pizza crust
1½ cups shredded pepper jack or Provolone cheese, divided
1 cup shredded rotisserie chicken breast, skin removed
2 tablespoons coarsely chopped parsley

8 SERVINGS

Salads
with Vegetables

Baby Spinach Chicken Walnut Salad

1 Arrange spinach in a large bowl or on a serving platter.

2 Top with chicken, oranges, walnuts, cheese and onion. Drizzle with dressing. Serve. Refrigerate leftovers.

Serve this luncheon salad with warm muffins or soft bakery rolls.

INGREDIENTS

8 cups baby spinach leaves
(about 6 ounces)
2 cups sliced rotisserie chicken,
skin removed
1 11-ounce can mandarin oranges,
drained
1 cup chopped walnuts, toasted
1 cup crumbled goat cheese
(about 4 ounces)
½ cup sliced red onion
½ cup light raspberry walnut
vinaigrette dressing

4 SERVINGS

Bacon and Chicken Caesar Salad

INGREDIENTS

2 cups shredded rotisserie chicken, skin removed
1 cup Parmesan ranch large-cut croutons
⅔ cup Caesar dressing
1 10-ounce bag romaine salad
5 slices fully cooked bacon, cut into 1-inch strips
¼ cup shredded Parmesan cheese

4 SERVINGS

1 Mix all ingredients except cheese in a large bowl. Divide into serving-size portions.

2 Sprinkle cheese on each salad when serving. Refrigerate leftovers.

Serve with crusty rolls.

Broccoli Avocado Chicken Salad

1 Place broccoli slaw, bell pepper, onions and chicken in a large bowl.

2 Mix olive oil, vinegar, salt and black pepper in a small bowl. Drizzle over salad and toss.

3 Gently stir in avocado just before serving. Refrigerate leftovers.

Serve with assorted crackers or breadsticks.

1 12-ounce package fresh broccoli slaw
⅔ cup chopped red bell pepper
½ cup minced red onion
2 cups diced rotisserie chicken breast, skin removed
¼ cup extra virgin olive oil, more if needed
¼ cup white balsamic vinegar
Salt and black pepper to taste
1 avocado, peeled, pitted and cubed

4 SERVINGS

Chef's Deluxe Salad

INGREDIENTS

1 small head iceberg lettuce, torn
  into pieces
2 cups bite-sized chunks of rotisserie
  chicken, skin removed
½ pound fully cooked ham, cut into
  thin strips
1 cup cubed Cheddar cheese
2 fresh tomatoes, cut into wedges
2 hard-boiled eggs, sliced
¾ cup French salad dressing

4 SERVINGS

1 Place all ingredients except salad dressing in a large salad bowl.

2 Toss with salad dressing just before serving. Refrigerate leftovers.

Serve with warm, crusty hard rolls.

Variation: This salad can be served as a side, with 6 portions, or as a 4-portion entrée.

Chipotle Chicken Salad

1 Shred chicken meat with your fingers; place in a large bowl. Add bell peppers, red onion, green onions and cilantro.

2 Mix mayonnaise, chipotles, lime juice, salt and black pepper in a small bowl. Add to chicken mixture; stir until coated.

3 Adjust seasoning, adding more salt, pepper and chopped chipotles, as desired. Chill. Serve. Refrigerate leftovers.

Serve on a bed of crisp lettuce along with warm, crusty rolls.

INGREDIENTS

1 rotisserie chicken, skin and
    bones discarded
Half of a red bell pepper, chopped
Half of a yellow bell pepper, chopped
1 small red onion, diced
2 green onions, thinly sliced
    diagonally
¼ cup chopped fresh cilantro
½ cup mayonnaise
¼ cup canned chipotles in adobo
    sauce, finely chopped, or to taste
1 tablespoon fresh lime juice
½ teaspoon sea salt, or to taste
⅛ teaspoon ground black pepper, or
    to taste

4 SERVINGS

Creamy German Chicken Salad

INGREDIENTS

½ pound mushrooms
1 to 2 tablespoons butter
4½ cups diced rotisserie chicken,
  skin removed
1½ cups chopped celery
1 cup mayonnaise
Salt and ground black pepper, to taste
1 cup heavy cream, whipped

6 SERVINGS

1 Sauté mushrooms in butter over medium heat in a skillet for about 2 to 3 minutes; remove with slotted spoon and place in a large bowl.

2 Add chicken, celery, mayonnaise, salt and pepper; stir to combine. Refrigerate and chill well.

3 Fold in whipped cream just before serving.

Serve over a bed of lettuce along with pumpernickel or rye bread.

Dilled Garden Salad with Chicken and Ham

1 Mix tomatoes, cucumber, onion and olives in a large serving bowl; toss.

2 Whisk together oil, vinegar, dill, salt, pepper and sugar in a small bowl. Pour over salad; toss. Chill well.

3 Stir in cheese, ham and chicken just before serving.

Serve this tasty salad along with warm hard rolls for a light lunch.

INGREDIENTS

2 medium-sized fresh tomatoes cut into bite-sized wedges
1 small cucumber, thinly sliced
1 small onion, halved lengthwise and thinly sliced crosswise
½ cup pitted Kalamata olives
¼ cup vegetable or olive oil
2 tablespoons white wine vinegar
1 to 2 tablespoons chopped fresh dill or 1 teaspoon dried dill weed
¼ teaspoon salt
¼ teaspoon black pepper
¼ teaspoon granulated sugar
4 ounces cubed mozzarella cheese
1 cup cubed fully cooked ham
1 cup cubed rotisserie chicken breast, skin removed

4 SERVINGS

Edamame and Herb Chicken Salad

INGREDIENTS

1 4-ounce package bagged salad mix
with herbs
1½ cups garlic flavor croutons
1 bunch fresh chives, chopped
Half of a large yellow bell pepper,
seeded and cut into thin strips
1 cup shelled edamame, thawed
if frozen
½ cup sliced green onions
½ cup toasted slivered almonds
3 cups cubed garlic flavor rotisserie
chicken, skin removed
½ cup Italian salad dressing, or to taste
Salt and black pepper to taste

6 SERVINGS

1 Toss all ingredients in a large salad bowl. Serve immediately on individual salad plates.

Who knew soybeans could be so tasty?

Variation: Serve with sliced romaine lettuce instead of herb salad.

Hot Chicken Salad

Preheat oven to 350°.

1 Mix celery, onion and bell pepper in a 1½-quart microwave-safe casserole. Cover; microwave on high for 1 to 2 minutes or until crisp-tender.

2 Stir in soup, mayonnaise, lemon juice and hot pepper sauce until blended. Stir in chicken and water chestnuts.

3 Bake, uncovered, for 15 minutes. Top with cheese; bake until hot and bubbly. Serve. Refrigerate leftovers.

Serve with soft bakery rolls.

 Tip: Cover and refrigerate up to 24 hours before baking.

INGREDIENTS

1½ cups sliced celery
¼ cup chopped yellow onion
1 red bell pepper, chopped
1 10.75-ounce can cream of
chicken soup
½ cup mayonnaise
3 tablespoons fresh lemon juice
¼ teaspoon hot pepper sauce
3 cups cubed rotisserie chicken,
skin removed
1 8-ounce can sliced water
chestnuts, drained
½ cup shredded Cheddar cheese

6 SERVINGS

Layered Chicken Taco Salad with Guacamole Dressing

INGREDIENTS

4 cups shredded iceberg lettuce
2 cups rotisserie chicken strips, skin removed
2 cups chopped fresh tomatoes
1 cup sliced black olives
2 green onions, chopped
2 medium avocados, peeled and pitted
¾ cup plain yogurt
3 tablespoons fresh lime juice
1 clove garlic, minced
1½ teaspoons chili powder
½ teaspoon salt
½ teaspoon ground cumin
Dash of hot pepper sauce
2 cups shredded taco cheese or shredded sharp Cheddar cheese

6 SERVINGS

1 Layer lettuce, chicken, tomato, olives and onions in a deep 3- or 4-quart glass dish with straight sides; set aside.

2 Puree avocados until smooth; spoon in a bowl. Add yogurt, lime juice, garlic, chili powder, salt, cumin and hot pepper sauce; mix well. Spread over onion layer. Top with cheese. Cover and chill before serving. Refrigerate leftovers.

Serve with tortilla chips.

Lentil and Couscous Chicken Salad

1 Bring lentils and 3 cups water to a boil in a small pot. Reduce heat, cover and simmer until tender but not falling apart, about 10 minutes. Drain and rinse with cold water; drain again.

2 Bring remaining ¾ cup water to a boil in a small pot. Pour over couscous in a large heatproof bowl; cover and set aside 10 minutes. Uncover and add olive oil; fluff with a fork. Let cool. Add cooked lentils, arugula, tomatoes and chicken. Toss to combine.

3 Whisk basil pesto, vinegar, salt and pepper in a small bowl. Drizzle over salad just before serving. Toss until coated. Serve. Refrigerate leftovers.

Serve this delicious salad for lunch or a light supper along with whole wheat rolls.

INGREDIENTS

¾ cup dried green lentils
3¾ cup water, divided
½ cup couscous (whole wheat or regular)
2 teaspoons extra virgin olive oil
2 cups, packed, baby arugula leaves
1 cup cherry tomatoes, halved
2 cups cubed rotisserie chicken breast, skin removed
¼ cup purchased basil pesto
1½ tablespoons red wine vinegar
¼ teaspoon salt
½ teaspoon black pepper

6 SERVINGS

Light Asian Cabbage Chicken Salad

INGREDIENTS

Dressing
⅓ cup granulated sugar
¾ teaspoon salt
½ teaspoon ground black pepper
⅓ cup cider vinegar
2 tablespoons vegetable oil

Salad
6 cups finely shredded cabbage
1½ cups cubed rotisserie chicken,
  skin removed
1 green onion, thinly sliced
1 3-ounce package ramen noodle
  soup mix, crumbled (discard
  seasoning packet)
3 tablespoons sliced or chopped
  almonds, toasted
2 teaspoons sesame seed, toasted

6 SERVINGS

1 Mix all dressing ingredients in a small bowl until blended.

2 Mix cabbage, chicken and onion in a large bowl.

3 Add crumbled ramen noodles, almonds and sesame seed to cabbage mixture. Add dressing; toss to coat. Serve. Refrigerate leftovers.

Serve with crunchy breadsticks and fresh melon wedges.

Polenta Zucchini Salad with Chicken

1 Cut zucchini in half lengthwise, then cut on the bias (diagonally) into ¼-inch-thick slices; place in a bowl and sprinkle with salt and pepper.

2 Heat ½ tablespoon olive oil in a large nonstick skillet over high heat. Add zucchini; cook and stir until just golden, about 2 minutes. Remove zucchini; set aside.

3 Reduce heat to medium. Add polenta to same skillet. Cook and stir until just heated through, about 4 minutes.

4 Whisk vinegar, oregano, sugar, salt and 3 tablespoons olive oil in a bowl.

5 In a large bowl, toss half the vinaigrette with the baby greens, chicken, zucchini and polenta. Arrange salad on a serving platter. Sprinkle with blue cheese. Serve with remaining vinaigrette. Refrigerate leftovers.

Purchased prepared polenta is used in this chicken salad.

Variation: Use baby arugula instead of baby mixed greens.

INGREDIENTS

2 small zucchinis
3½ tablespoons extra virgin olive oil, divided
Half of a 16-ounce package prepared polenta, cut into ¾-inch cubes
2 tablespoons red wine vinegar
1 tablespoon chopped fresh oregano
½ teaspoon granulated sugar
½ teaspoon salt
5 cups baby mixed greens
2 boneless, skinless rotisserie chicken breasts, shredded
½ cup (3 ounces) crumbled blue cheese

4 SERVINGS

Quinoa Salad with Chicken

INGREDIENTS

1 ⅓ cups uncooked quinoa
2 cups water
Pinch of salt
2 tablespoons white wine vinegar
2 tablespoons olive oil
Salt and pepper to taste
2 cups shredded rotisserie chicken,
  skin removed
1 ½ cups green grapes, quartered
½ cup sliced almonds, toasted
Lettuce

4 SERVINGS

1 Rinse quinoa under cold running water and drain. Bring 2 cups water to a boil. Stir in quinoa and a pinch of salt. Reduce heat, cover and simmer until tender and most of the liquid is absorbed, about 15 to 20 minutes. Uncover and let cool; set aside.

2 Whisk vinegar, oil, salt and pepper in a large bowl until blended. Add quinoa; toss to combine. Add chicken, grapes and almonds; toss. Serve over lettuce, at room temperature or chilled.

Serve this main course salad along with sliced tomatoes and cucumbers.

Sausage and Chicken Rice Salad

1 Mix first seven ingredients in a large bowl. Add salad dressing, salt and pepper to taste; toss to coat.

2 Serve salad over shredded spinach on individual salad plates; sprinkle each serving with nuts. Refrigerate leftovers.

Serve this main dish salad along with fresh sliced tomatoes and crisp breadsticks.

Variation: Use cooked, smoked sausage.

INGREDIENTS

2 cups cooked rice
1 pound chorizo sausage, cooked and
   thinly sliced
1½ cups diced rotisserie chicken,
   skin removed
1 cup thinly sliced red onion
1 cup cherry tomato halves
1 cup shredded carrots
2 tablespoons minced flat leaf parsley
¾ cup purchased Vidalia onion
   vinaigrette salad dressing
Salt and black pepper to taste
1 10-ounce bag spinach, shredded
¾ cup honey roasted sunflower nuts
   or pecans

4 SERVINGS

Tossed Taco Salad

INGREDIENTS

Dressing
½ cup mayonnaise
½ cup French dressing
½ cup whole milk
Half of a 1.25-ounce package taco
    seasoning mix

Salad
7 cups chopped iceberg lettuce
1 cup chopped yellow onion
1 green bell pepper, chopped
2 large fresh tomatoes, chopped
½ pound ground beef, fully cooked,
    crumbled and well drained
2 cups shredded rotisserie chicken,
    skin removed
1 15-ounce can kidney beans, drained
2 cups grated Cheddar cheese
Half of a 15-ounce bag tortilla chips,
    slightly crushed

4 SERVINGS

Dressing

1 Mix dressing ingredients until combined.

Salad

1 Combine all salad ingredients in a large bowl; toss with dressing.
Refrigerate leftovers.

Rotisserie chicken and ground beef fill this tasty salad bowl.

Salads with Pasta, Rice & Couscous

Ali's Favorite Pasta Salad

INGREDIENTS

1 package ranch and bacon pasta
   salad mix
½ cup frozen peas
½ cup mayonnaise
2 cups cubed rotisserie chicken,
   skin removed
1 cup cherry tomatoes, halved
½ cup cubed Cheddar cheese
Shredded iceberg lettuce
4 green onions, chopped

6 SERVINGS

1 Fill a 3-quart pot two-thirds full with water. Bring water to a boil over high heat. Add pasta from the salad-mix package. Reduce heat to medium and cook, uncovered, for 12 minutes, stirring occasionally. Add peas to the pot for the last 3 minutes of cooking time. Drain pasta and peas. Rinse with cold water, then drain well again.

2 Stir mayonnaise and contents of the salad-mix seasoning packet together in a large bowl. Add cooked pasta and peas, chicken, tomatoes and cheese; mix well.

3 Cover and chill in the refrigerator. Serve chilled, over shredded iceberg lettuce and topped with green onions. Refrigerate leftovers.

Serve with warm French bread or crusty rolls.

Black-Eyed Pea Chicken Pasta Salad

1 Cook pasta according to package instructions. Rinse with cold water; drain.

2 Mix cooked pasta and remaining salad ingredients in a large bowl.

3 Mix all dressing ingredients in small jar with tight-fitting lid; shake well. Pour dressing over salad; toss to coat. Chill. Serve. Refrigerate leftovers.

*Do not touch your eyes when working with jalapeños!

Serve this luncheon salad over lettuce along with warm French bread.

Variation: Use purchased Italian salad dressing.

INGREDIENTS

Salad
2 cups (8 ounces) uncooked dried spiral pasta
1 15-ounce can black-eyed peas, rinsed and drained
1 medium yellow bell pepper, cut into ¼-inch pieces
1 cup small grape tomatoes
½ cup sliced green onions
4 ounces (1 cup) mild Cheddar cheese, cut into ½-inch cubes
2 cups finely-cubed rotisserie chicken breast, skin removed

Dressing
¼ cup extra virgin olive oil
¼ cup freshly squeezed lime juice
2 tablespoons finely chopped jalapeño chile pepper (seeds removed)*
3 tablespoons chopped fresh cilantro or flat leaf parsley
1 teaspoon finely chopped fresh garlic
1 teaspoon granulated sugar
1 teaspoon salt
¼ teaspoon ground black pepper

4 SERVINGS

BLT and Chicken Pasta Salad

INGREDIENTS

1½ cups uncooked orzo pasta
2 cups cubed rotisserie chicken,
  skin removed
2 cups halved grape tomatoes
2 cups thinly sliced leaf lettuce
  or spinach
½ cup thinly sliced green onions
4 slices crisply cooked bacon,
  crumbled
3 tablespoons olive oil
1½ tablespoons white wine vinegar
½ tablespoon Dijon mustard
Salt and black pepper to taste

4 SERVINGS

1 Cook pasta according to package directions; rinse with cold water until cool and drain. Mix cooled pasta, chicken, tomatoes, lettuce, onions and bacon in a large bowl.

2 Whisk remaining ingredients in a small bowl. Pour over salad and toss gently to coat. Serve. Refrigerate leftovers.

If you enjoy a bacon, lettuce and tomato sandwich, you will love this salad.

Bow Tie Pasta Salad with Walnut Pesto

1 Mix cooked pasta, chicken, tomatoes and olives in a large bowl.

2 Add all pesto ingredients in a food processor; pulse until finely minced; add mixture to pasta mixture. Toss to coat. Serve immediately. Refrigerate leftovers.

Serve over lettuce along with warm, crusty rolls.

INGREDIENTS

2 cups bow tie pasta, cooked, drained and rinsed in cold water
2 cups cubed rotisserie chicken breast, skin removed
1 cup quartered fresh cherry tomatoes
2 tablespoons chopped pitted Kalamata olives

Pesto
1 cup fresh basil leaves
½ cup fresh parsley
3 tablespoons coarsely chopped walnuts, toasted
1½ tablespoons extra virgin olive oil
1 tablespoon white wine vinegar
½ teaspoon salt
1 garlic clove

4 SERVINGS

Caesar Chicken Pasta Salad

INGREDIENTS

3 cups cooked penne (about 6 ounces
   uncooked)
3 cups shredded rotisserie chicken
   breast, skin removed
2 cups thinly sliced romaine lettuce
1 ½ cups halved cherry tomatoes
½ cup thinly sliced fresh basil
½ cup chopped green onions
¼ cup chopped flat leaf parsley
1 garlic clove, minced
1 4-ounce package crumbled
   feta cheese
⅓ cup fat-free Caesar dressing
Salt and black pepper to taste

4 SERVINGS

1 Add all ingredients to a large bowl; toss to coat well. Serve.
Refrigerate leftovers.

Serve with warm, crusty bread.

 Variation: Use other type cheese.

Cherry Chicken Buffet Pasta Salad

1 Cook pasta according to package directions. Rinse with cold water; drain. Place in a large bowl. Add chicken, celery, onion and cherries.

2 In a small bowl, mix mayonnaise, poppy seed dressing, salt and pepper. Fold 1¾ cups dressing mixture into salad, reserving ¾ cup. Cover and refrigerate several hours or overnight

3 To serve, fold in spinach and walnuts; add reserved dressing mixture as needed. Spoon salad into a lettuce-lined serving dish. Refrigerate leftovers.

This salad makes 16 1-cup buffet servings.

Variation: Use to make 8 2-cup luncheon servings.

INGREDIENTS

1 16-ounce package dry gnocchi or
   shell pasta
4 cups cubed rotisserie chicken,
   skin removed
¾ cup thinly sliced celery
¾ cup chopped red onion
1 5-ounce package dried cherries
1¼ cups mayonnaise
1¼ cups creamy style poppy
   seed dressing
½ teaspoons salt, or to taste
¼ teaspoon ground black pepper
4 cups baby spinach, stems removed
1 cup chopped walnuts, toasted
Curly leaf lettuce

16 SERVINGS

Chicken and Soba Noodle Salad

INGREDIENTS

3 ounces uncooked soba noodles
(buckwheat noodles)
1 8-ounce steam-and-serve package
sugar snap peas
1 red bell pepper, thinly sliced
lengthwise
3 cups shredded lemon-pepper
rotisserie chicken, skin removed
½ cup light sesame-ginger salad
dressing
Shredded napa cabbage (Chinese
cabbage)
Toasted sesame seeds
Sliced green onions

4 SERVINGS

1 Cook soba noodles according to package directions. Drain.

2 Microwave peas in package on high for 1 minute. Rinse peas with cold water; drain.

3 Mix peas, noodles, bell pepper, chicken and salad dressing in a large bowl; toss.

4 Serve over shredded cabbage. Garnish with sesame seeds and green onions as desired. Serve. Refrigerate leftovers.

Serve this Asian-style salad with crisp breadsticks for a delicious lunch.

Chicken Pasta Salad with Special Oriental Dressing

1 Cook pasta according to package directions; drain.

2 Mix cooked pasta, chicken, green onions, carrot and pimento in a large bowl.

Dressing

1 Mix dressing ingredients in a small bowl until blended. Pour over chicken mixture; toss. Serve warm or chilled. Refrigerate leftovers.

Serve this colorful, flavorful salad on a bed of lettuce along with warm rolls.

INGREDIENTS

1 12-ounce package rainbow pasta twists
2 skinless, boneless rotisserie chicken breasts, cut into thin strips
4 green onions, sliced
1 medium carrot, shredded
1 2-ounce jar diced pimento, drained

Dressing
6 tablespoons low-sodium soy sauce
⅓ cup reduced-sodium chicken broth
1 tablespoon sesame oil
1 clove garlic, finely chopped
¼ teaspoon ground ginger
⅛ teaspoon crushed red pepper

6 SERVINGS

Curried Chicken Rice Salad

INGREDIENTS

1 package (6.9 ounces) chicken-flavored rice-vermicelli mix, such as Rice-a-Roni®

1 8-ounce jar marinated artichoke hearts

4 green onions, chopped

Half of a green bell pepper, chopped

½ cup sliced celery

1 cup pitted black olives, sliced

1 8-ounce can water chestnuts, drained

2 cups chopped rotisserie chicken, skin removed

½ cup mayonnaise

1 teaspoon curry powder, or to taste

Salt and black pepper to taste

4 SERVINGS

1 Cook rice-vermicelli mix according to package directions.

2 Drain artichokes, reserving marinade; chop and place in a large bowl. Add onions, bell pepper, celery, olives, water chestnuts, chicken and cooked rice-vermicelli mix.

3 Mix mayonnaise, curry powder and reserved marinade in a small bowl; pour over rice mixture and stir until well mixed. Season with salt and pepper to taste. Serve warm or cold. Refrigerate leftovers.

Serve this salad for lunch or a light supper along with a side of fresh sliced tomatoes and warm rolls.

Ham and Chicken Pasta Salad

1 Mix cooked pasta, ham, chicken, tomatoes and green onions in a large bowl.

2 Mix dressing, dill and black pepper in a small bowl; pour over pasta mixture and toss. Sprinkle cheese over mixture; toss. Serve immediately or chill. Refrigerate leftovers.

Serve this quick and tasty salad on a bed of lettuce along with buttered corn on the cob and hard rolls.

INGREDIENTS

1½ cups (6 ounces) small shell or elbow pasta, cooked and drained
1 cup diced fully cooked ham
1½ cups diced rotisserie chicken breast, skin removed
1 cup halved cherry tomatoes
½ cup sliced green onions
½ cup ranch or creamy Italian dressing, or to taste
1 tablespoon chopped fresh dill or ½ teaspoon dried dill
½ teaspoon ground black pepper
6 slices deli-style sliced sharp Cheddar cheese, cut into ½-inch wide strips

4 SERVINGS

Italian Sub Chicken Pasta Salad with Broccoli

INGREDIENTS

3 cups cooked whole wheat fusilli
  pasta or pasta of your choice
2 cups steamed broccoli
1 cup halved cherry tomatoes
8 button mushrooms, cleaned
  and quartered
6 slices salami cut into strips
6 slices provolone cheese cut
  into strips
½ rotisserie chicken breast, skin
  removed, cut into thin strips
Italian dressing to taste

4 SERVINGS

1 Mix first seven ingredients in a large bowl. Add dressing; toss gently to combine. Serve on lettuce-lined salad plates. Refrigerate leftovers.

Serve this delicious sub salad with crusty Italian bread.

Macaroni Chicken Salad

1 Cook pasta according to package directions; drain and rinse with cold water until cool; drain again. Set aside.

2 Gently mix all ingredients in a large bowl. Serve chilled or at room temperature. Refrigerate leftovers.

Serve this simple salad with a side of sliced fresh tomatoes and crusty rolls.

INGREDIENTS

8 ounces elbow macaroni
⅓ cup Italian salad dressing
½ cup mayonnaise, more if needed
1 cup cubed Cheddar cheese
½ cup chopped celery
½ cup diced green bell pepper
¼ cup chopped yellow onion
2 cups cubed rotisserie chicken breast, skin removed
Salt and black pepper to taste

4 SERVINGS

Party Chicken Pasta Salad

INGREDIENTS

16 ounces uncooked rotini pasta
1 large green bell pepper, diced
1 large red bell pepper, diced
1 medium zucchini, cut crosswise into
   ¼-inch slices, then quartered
1 medium yellow summer squash,
   cut crosswise into ¼-inch slices,
   then quartered
1 8-ounce package button
   mushrooms, sliced
½ cup chopped green onions
1 cup finely chopped flat leaf parsley
4 cups diced rotisserie chicken,
   skin removed
1½ cups mayonnaise
1 8-ounce container plain yogurt
1 tablespoon fresh lemon juice
1 teaspoon salt, or to taste
½ teaspoon ground black pepper
2 cloves fresh garlic, minced
½ cup freshly grated Parmesan cheese
Curly leaf lettuce
4 fresh tomatoes, cut into wedges

16 (1-CUP) SERVINGS

1 Cook pasta according to package directions. Drain and rinse with cold water; drain again.

2 Place cooked, cooled pasta, bell peppers, zucchini, yellow squash, mushrooms, onions, parsley and chicken in large bowl.

3 Mix remaining ingredients except lettuce and tomatoes in a small bowl; pour over salad and toss to coat. Cover and refrigerate. When serving, line a serving platter with lettuce. Spoon salad over lettuce. Garnish edges with tomato wedges. Refrigerate leftovers.

Perfect for bridal or baby showers. Serve with assorted fresh fruit, soft rolls or croissants.

Pasta Chicken Club Salad

1 Toss pasta with chicken, bacon and dressing in a large bowl. Chill.

2 Just before serving, toss pasta mixture with tomatoes and 1 cup cheese.

3 Arrange salad greens on individual serving plates. Top each equally with pasta mixture. Sprinkle with remaining cheese. Serve. Refrigerate leftovers.

Club salad is always a favorite . . . serve with crusty rolls.

INGREDIENTS

12 ounces spiral or tube pasta, cooked according to package directions; drained
3 cups diced rotisserie chicken, skin removed
8 strips bacon, crisply cooked, crumbled
1 cup ranch salad dressing
2 large tomatoes, seeded and chopped
1½ cups shredded double Cheddar cheese, divided
1 10-ounce package salad greens

4 SERVINGS

Pasta with Chicken and Creamy Sun-Dried Tomato Sauce

INGREDIENTS

3 cups dried farfalle pasta
3 tablespoons sun-dried tomato pesto
2 tablespoons crème fraiche
Salt and black pepper to taste
2 cups shredded rotisserie chicken,
   skin removed

2 SERVINGS

1 Cook pasta according to package directions; drain well and return hot pasta to pot.

2 Add pesto, crème fraiche and salt and pepper to taste. Stir gently to blend. Add chicken; toss to coat. Serve. Refrigerate leftovers.

Serve with hard rolls and a side of assorted roasted vegetables.

 Tip: Double the recipe for delicious leftovers.

Ramen Noodles Chicken Salad

1 Heat olive oil in a large skillet over medium heat. Break noodles into bite-sized pieces; add to skillet along with contents of seasoning packet. Cook and stir 2 minutes. Add sesame seeds; cook and stir 2 minutes or until noodles and seeds are golden brown.

2 Mix sugar, vinegar, vegetable oil and black pepper in a large bowl until blended.

3 Add chicken, peanuts, green onions and coleslaw mix. Add browned noodle mixture including olive oil. Toss gently until combined. Serve. Refrigerate leftovers.

Serve this crunchy main dish salad for lunch or a light supper.

INGREDIENTS

3 tablespoons olive oil
1 3-ounce package Oriental flavor
  ramen noodle soup mix
2 tablespoons sesame seeds
¼ cup granulated sugar
¼ cup white wine vinegar
1 tablespoon vegetable oil
¼ teaspoon black pepper
2 cups coarsely diced rotisserie
  chicken breast, skin removed
½ cup roasted peanuts
4 green onions, sliced
1 1-pound bag coleslaw mix

4 SERVINGS

Southwestern Pasta Salad with Chicken

INGREDIENTS

8 ounces uncooked rotini pasta
⅓ cup corn oil
¼ cup fresh lime juice
2 tablespoons chili powder, or to taste
2 teaspoons ground cumin
½ teaspoon salt
2 cloves garlic, crushed
1½ cups whole kernel corn
1 15-ounce can black beans, rinsed
   and drained
½ cup diced green bell pepper
¼ cup fresh cilantro leaves, divided
2½ cups diced rotisserie chicken,
   skin removed
Lettuce
1 cup chopped Roma (plum) tomatoes

4 SERVINGS

1 Cook pasta in lightly salted boiling water about 8 to 10 minutes or to al dente; drain.

2 In a large bowl, mix corn oil, lime juice, chili powder, cumin salt and garlic. Stir in cooked pasta; cool to room temperature, stirring occasionally.

3 Stir in remaining ingredients except tomatoes. Spoon onto a serving platter lined with lettuce. Garnish with tomatoes. Serve. Refrigerate leftovers.

Serve with warm corn muffins or flour tortillas along with fresh fruit.

Spaghetti Chicken Salad

1 Cook pasta according to package directions; drain well. Toss with ½ cup salad dressing. Cool.

2 Add remaining ingredients, including remaining salad dressing. Mix well. Chill before serving. Refrigerate leftovers.

Serve this simple main dish salad with crusty rolls.

1 16-ounce package thin spaghetti
1 8-ounce bottle ranch salad dressing, divided
2 cups diced rotisserie chicken breast, skin removed
½ pound thinly sliced salami, cut into strips
4 hard-boiled eggs, chopped
2 medium tomatoes, seeded and coarsely chopped
1 cucumber, seeded and chopped
4 large stalks celery, thinly sliced
1 cup thinly sliced green onions including tops
Salt and pepper to taste

4 SERVINGS

Three-Cheese Tortellini Chicken Pasta Salad

INGREDIENTS

1 9-ounce package refrigerated
  three-cheese tortellini
1 7-ounce container refrigerated
  pesto with basil
3 tablespoons cider vinegar
½ teaspoon seasoned salt
¼ teaspoon granulated sugar
⅛ teaspoon ground black pepper
3 cups rotisserie chicken breast, skin
  removed, cut into strips
½ cup chopped red bell pepper
1½ cups fresh zucchini, sliced and cut
  into quarters

6 SERVINGS

1 Cook tortellini according to package directions; rinse with cold water and drain.

2 Whisk pesto, vinegar, seasoned salt, sugar and black pepper in large salad bowl until well blended. Add remaining ingredients; mix to coat well. Serve. Refrigerate leftovers.

Using refrigerated pasta and prepared pesto is a simple way to prepare a delicious meal for family or friends. Serve with green salad and warm Italian bread.

Thai Chicken Fettuccine Salad

1 Heat picante sauce, peanut butter, honey, orange juice, soy sauce and ginger in a 10-inch nonstick skillet over medium heat until mixture is hot and bubbly.

2 Add chicken; cook 1 minute. Add cooked fettuccine; toss until coated.

3 Serve over mixed salad greens; garnish each serving equally with red bell pepper and chopped cilantro. Refrigerate leftovers.

Serve this sweet and spicy salad with crisp breadsticks.

INGREDIENTS

1 cup purchased picante sauce
¼ cup chunky peanut butter
2 tablespoons honey
2 tablespoons fresh orange juice
1 teaspoon soy sauce
½ teaspoon ground ginger
2 cups cubed rotisserie chicken, skin removed
6 ounces fettuccine, cooked according to package directions, then drained
4 cups mixed salad greens
½ cup chopped red bell pepper
¼ cup chopped fresh cilantro leaves

4 SERVINGS

Tomato Basil Pasta Salad with Mozzarella and Chicken

INGREDIENTS

3 ounces uncooked angel hair pasta, broken into thirds

¼ cup chopped fresh basil leaves

4 medium Roma (plum) tomatoes cut into ¼-inch slices

4 ounces (1 cup) mozzarella cheese cut into ½-inch cubes

2 cups finely cubed rotisserie chicken breast, skin removed

¼ cup extra virgin olive oil

¼ cup red wine vinegar or cider vinegar

2 teaspoons granulated sugar

1 teaspoon finely chopped fresh garlic

⅛ teaspoon salt

⅛ teaspoon ground black pepper

4 SERVINGS

1 Cook pasta according to package directions. Drain and rinse with cold water; drain. Place in a large bowl with basil, tomatoes, cheese and chicken.

2 Whisk remaining ingredients in a small bowl until blended. Pour dressing over salad and gently stir to coat. Refrigerate leftovers.

Serve over leaf lettuce, along with warm Italian bread.

Veggies and Chicken Pasta Salad

1 Cook pasta according to package directions. Drain and rinse in cold water to cool; drain.

2 Mix cooled pasta and remaining ingredients in a large bowl. Stir gently to coat. Cover and chill slightly. Refrigerate leftovers.

This is a great salad for the whole family. Serve with rolls or crispy breadsticks.

INGREDIENTS

4 cups uncooked medium shell pasta
4 cups cubed rotisserie chicken, skin removed
1 16-ounce package frozen mixed vegetables, cooked and drained
½ cup thinly sliced celery
½ cup finely chopped onion
1 8-ounce bottle ranch salad dressing
½ teaspoon salt or to taste
½ teaspoon dill weed
¼ teaspoon ground black pepper or to taste
1 cup shredded Cheddar cheese

6 SERVINGS

Warm Chicken and Couscous Salad

INGREDIENTS

1½ cups water
1 cup instant couscous
¾ teaspoon salt
2 carrots, peeled and chopped
2 green onions, chopped
⅓ cup dried cranberries
¼ cup extra virgin olive oil
2 tablespoons sherry vinegar
Ground black pepper to taste
Salt to taste
2 cups thinly sliced rotisserie chicken
   breast, skin removed
1 tablespoon thinly sliced fresh mint

6 SERVINGS

1 Bring water to a boil in a small saucepan over high heat. Stir in couscous and salt. Return to a boil. Remove from heat. Cover and let stand 5 minutes; remove from saucepan and place in a bowl. Fluff with a fork.

2 Add carrots, onions and cranberries.

3 Whisk olive oil and vinegar in a small bowl. Season with black pepper and salt to taste. Stir into the couscous mixture and place in a serving dish. Arrange chicken on top. Sprinkle with mint. Serve warm. Refrigerate leftovers.

Couscous is a granular pasta made from durum wheat flour.

Serve this main dish salad for a light super.

Warm Pesto Chicken Pasta Salad

1 Cook pasta according to package directions; drain and set aside.

2 Spray a nonstick skillet lightly with cooking spray. Add chicken and tomatoes; cook and stir 2 minutes. Add pesto; stir until heated through. Add cooked pasta; toss to coat. Sprinkle with nuts. Serve. Refrigerate leftovers.

Prepared pesto and rotisserie chicken make this a quick and easy warm salad. Serve with a spinach salad and warm hard rolls.

INGREDIENTS

1 16-ounce package spiral pasta
2 cups cubed rotisserie chicken breast, skin removed
1 cup chopped fresh tomatoes
1 7-ounce container prepared pesto
¼ cup toasted pine nuts or chopped walnuts

4 SERVINGS

Zesty Pasta Salad
with Black Beans and Chicken

INGREDIENTS

1 7-ounce package spiral pasta
2 15-ounce cans black beans, rinsed
and drained
2½ cups small-diced rotisserie chicken
breast, skin removed
2 fresh tomatoes, seeded and
chopped
1 cup Italian salad dressing, or to taste
Salt and black pepper to taste

4 SERVINGS

1 Cook pasta according to package directions; drain, rinse in cold water and drain again. Place in a large bowl.

2 Add beans, chicken and tomatoes to pasta bowl. Drizzle with salad dressing. Season with salt and black pepper to taste. Toss to coat. Cover and chill. Serve. Refrigerate leftovers.

Serve this special salad over a bed of fresh salad greens along with soft breadsticks.

Salads with Fruit

Apple Walnut Chicken Salad

INGREDIENTS

Salad

6 cups mixed field greens (such as arugula, radicchio, curly endive)
2½ cups shredded rotisserie chicken breast, skin removed
⅓ cup blue cheese, crumbled
½ cup toasted chopped walnuts
2 ounces apple chips

Dressing

2 tablespoons apple juice concentrate
1 tablespoon apple cider vinegar
1 tablespoon white balsamic vinegar
1 teaspoon Dijon mustard
¼ teaspoon garlic powder
⅓ cup extra virgin olive oil

6 SERVINGS

1 Place all salad ingredients in a large bowl.

2 Whisk all dressing ingredients in a small bowl; add to salad mixture and toss. Serve immediately. Refrigerate leftovers.

Apple chips are the mystery ingredient in this main course salad. Serve with warm apple muffins or soft bakery rolls.

Blueberry Chicken Salad

1 Mix chicken, blueberries and almonds in a large bowl.

2 Mix remaining ingredients in a small bowl until blended. Stir mixture into chicken mixture. Chill. Serve on leaf lettuce. Refrigerate leftovers.

Serve this luncheon salad with assorted warm muffins and breads.

Recipe adapted from my book, *The Joy of Blueberries*.

INGREDIENTS

4 cups diced rotisserie chicken breast, skin removed
1 cup dried blueberries
½ cup toasted slivered almonds
½ cup mayonnaise
¼ cup sour cream
1 tablespoon fresh lemon juice
¼ cup chutney
¼ teaspoon salt
¼ teaspoon salt
⅛ teaspoon ground black pepper
Leaf lettuce

6 SERVINGS

Blue Cheese and Grape Chicken Salad

INGREDIENTS

2 small heads Boston lettuce, torn
  into pieces
4 stalks celery, sliced diagonally
Half of a red onion, finely chopped
2 cups green grapes, halved
3 ounces blue cheese, crumbled
2 tablespoons fresh lemon juice
2 tablespoons white wine vinegar
⅓ cup extra virgin olive oil
½ teaspoon kosher salt
¼ teaspoon freshly ground black
  pepper
1 rotisserie chicken, skin and bones
  removed, thickly sliced

4 SERVINGS

1 Mix lettuce, celery, onion, grapes and cheese in a large bowl.

2 Whisk lemon juice, vinegar, olive oil, salt and pepper in a
small bowl.

3 Portion equal amounts of salad and chicken on individual salad
plates. Serve with vinaigrette on the side. Refrigerate leftovers.

Serve with warm hard rolls.

 Variation: Use Bibb lettuce instead of Boston lettuce.

California Classic Chicken Salad

1 Place first four ingredients in a large bowl.

2 Mix all dressing ingredients in a small bowl until blended. Add to chicken salad and gently stir to coat well. Chill slightly before serving. Refrigerate leftovers.

Serve over a bed of lettuce along with warm hard rolls.

Variation: Serve in pita bread or over croissants.

INGREDIENTS

3 cups bite-sized diced rotisserie
   chicken breast, skin removed
1 cup toasted pecan pieces
2 cups red seedless grapes
3 stalks celery, very thinly sliced

Dressing
1 cup mayonnaise
4 teaspoons apple cider vinegar
5 teaspoons honey
2 teaspoons poppy seed
Salt and freshly ground pepper
   to taste

6 SERVINGS

Cashew and Grape Chicken Salad

INGREDIENTS

Salad

1½ cups cashews, roasted and salted
3 cups finely cubed rotisserie chicken, skin removed
¼ cup green onions, thinly sliced
1½ cups seedless grapes

Dressing

3 tablespoons soy sauce
2 tablespoons corn oil
2 tablespoons honey
1 tablespoon sesame oil
¼ teaspoon crushed red pepper flakes

4 SERVINGS

1 Mix all salad ingredients in a large salad bowl.

2 Mix all dressing ingredients in a small bowl until blended; pour over salad ingredients and toss to coat. Serve. Refrigerate leftovers.

Serve this entrée salad over a bed of mixed greens.

Serve along with poppy seed muffins or soft breadsticks.

Chicken Peach Salad

1 Place all salad ingredients in a large serving bowl.

2 Whisk all dressing ingredients in a small bowl. Drizzle over salad and toss. Serve. Refrigerate leftovers.

Serve with buttered croissants or soft bakery rolls.

Recipe adapted from my book, *The Joy of Peaches*.

INGREDIENTS

Salad
2 heads romaine lettuce, cut crosswise into 1-inch strips
3 cups rotisserie chicken breast, skin removed, sliced into thick ½-inch-wide strips
3 ripe peaches, peeled, pitted and coarsely chopped
¾ cup (3 ounces) blue cheese, crumbled
½ cup almonds, coarsely chopped

Dressing
¼ cup white wine vinegar
¼ cup extra virgin olive oil
1 teaspoon salt
¼ teaspoon freshly ground black pepper

6 SERVINGS

Curried Chicken
and Mango Salad

INGREDIENTS

4 cups diced rotisserie chicken,
   skin removed
1 cup chopped, roasted and salted
   cashews
4 green onions, thinly sliced
2 mangoes, peeled, cored and cut
   into ½-inch cubes
2 stalks celery, chopped
2 tablespoons fresh lemon juice
¼ cup mayonnaise
¼ cup plain yogurt
1½ teaspoons curry powder
½ teaspoon ground cumin
6 lettuce leaves
2 tablespoons chopped fresh cilantro

6 SERVINGS

1 Mix first six ingredients in a large bowl.

2 Mix mayonnaise, yogurt, curry powder and cumin in a small bowl; stir mixture into chicken mixture until coated. Serve over lettuce leaves and garnish with cilantro. Serve. Refrigerate leftovers.

Serve with crisp cheese-flavored breadsticks.

Festive Chicken Salad with Cranberries and Pecans

1 Mix mayonnaise, paprika and salt in a medium bowl. Stir in cranberries, celery, onion, bell pepper and pecans until blended.

2 Add chicken and black pepper to taste; mix well. Chill before serving. Refrigerate leftovers.

This is a nice salad to serve for the holidays.

Serve in lettuce cups or fresh tomato cups, along with soft rolls.

Variation: Use as sandwich filling.

INGREDIENTS

1 cup mayonnaise
1 teaspoon paprika
1 teaspoon seasoned salt
1½ cups dried cranberries
1 cup chopped celery
2 green onions, chopped
½ cup minced green bell pepper
1 cup chopped pecans
4 cups cubed rotisserie chicken, skin removed
¼ teaspoon ground black pepper, or to taste

6 SERVINGS

Fruit and Chicken Salad

INGREDIENTS

1 8-ounce container lemon yogurt
2 tablespoons honey
1 teaspoon grated orange peel
2 cups cubed rotisserie chicken breast,
  skin removed
1 cup seedless red grapes, halved
½ cup thinly sliced celery
3 tablespoons coarsely chopped
  walnuts
Boston or Bibb lettuce
2 apples, cored and cut into thin
  wedges

4 SERVINGS

1 Mix yogurt, honey and grated orange peel in a small bowl;
set aside.

2 Mix chicken, grapes, celery and walnuts in a medium serving
bowl. Add yogurt mixture; toss gently until coated.

3 Line 4 individual salad plates with lettuce; arrange apple slices
equally over lettuce. Spoon chicken mixture over apples.
Sprinkle each salad with additional walnuts as desired. Serve.

This is a quick and delicious luncheon salad. Serve with assorted
warm muffins.

Jerk Chicken and Mango Salad

1 Toss all ingredients except almonds and greens in a medium bowl.

2 Place greens in 4 salad bowls. Top equally with chicken mixture. Sprinkle equally with almonds. Serve. Refrigerate leftovers.

Serve this tasty luncheon salad with assorted crackers.

INGREDIENTS

2 cups diced rotisserie chicken, skin removed
1 cup bite-sized pieces fresh mango
⅔ cup lime vinaigrette salad dressing
½ cup small slivers of red onion
1 teaspoon jerk seasoning
¼ cup toasted slivered almonds
6 cups spring mix greens

4 SERVINGS

Louisiana Toasted Pecan Chicken Salad

INGREDIENTS

3 cups bite-sized shredded rotisserie
  chicken, skin removed
1 cup pecan pieces, toasted
1 cup halved red grapes
1 cup coarsely chopped celery
¾ cup mayonnaise, more if needed
2 tablespoons whole milk
1 teaspoon dried parsley flakes,
  optional
Salt and black pepper to taste
Lettuce

6 SERVINGS

1 Mix chicken, pecans, grapes and celery in a large bowl.

2 Mix remaining ingredients except lettuce in a small bowl. Gently stir mayonnaise mixture into chicken mixture until well combined. Chill before serving. Serve over a bed of lettuce. Refrigerate leftovers.

Serve this delicious salad for a no-cook lunch or a light evening meal, along with warm, crusty rolls or breadsticks.

Mandarin Chicken Salad

1 Mix salad dressing and marmalade in a large bowl until well blended.

2 Add chicken, onion and salad greens; toss to coat. Gently fold in oranges and croutons. Serve. Refrigerate leftovers.

Sliced chicken breast is featured in this tasty salad. Serve with warm muffins or crusty bread.

INGREDIENTS

½ cup ranch salad dressing
¼ cup orange marmalade
3 cups sliced rotisserie chicken breast, skin removed
¼ cup thinly sliced red onion
4 cups mixed salad greens
1 11-ounce can Mandarin oranges, drained
½ cup seasoned croutons

4 SERVINGS

Pacific Rim Chicken Salad

INGREDIENTS

1 16-ounce bag coleslaw mix
2 cups shredded rotisserie chicken,
 skin removed
1 cup diced mango
¾ cup Oriental salad dressing
½ cup slivered red bell pepper
½ cup toasted slivered almonds

6 SERVINGS

3 Place all ingredients in a large salad bowl; toss. Chill 15 minutes before serving. Refrigerate leftovers.

Serve with assorted crisp crackers or hard rolls.

Pineapple Mango Chicken Salad

1 Place all ingredients except chow mein noodles in a large bowl. Stir gently until coated. Chill slightly before serving. Sprinkle with noodles when serving. Refrigerate leftovers.

Serve over leaf lettuce along with warm muffins or soft bakery rolls.

Variation: Sprinkle with toasted slivered almonds instead of noodles.

INGREDIENTS

1 20-ounce can pineapple tidbits, drained
1 11-ounce can mandarin oranges, drained
1 mango, peeled and cut into small cubes
4 cups cubed rotisserie chicken, skin removed
1 cup salad dressing or mayonnaise
1 tablespoon prepared mustard
1 cup chopped celery
½ cup chopped green bell pepper
2 tablespoons grated yellow onion
¼ teaspoon salt
⅛ teaspoon ground black pepper
1 5-ounce can chow mein noodles

6 SERVINGS

Pineapple and Papaya
Curried Chicken Pasta Salad

INGREDIENTS

1 cup uncooked rotini pasta
1 small pineapple
1 small papaya
5 cups shredded romaine lettuce
1½ cups cubed rotisserie chicken,
   skin removed

Dressing
½ cup light mayonnaise
1 tablespoon honey
1 tablespoon rice vinegar or
   white vinegar
1 teaspoon curry powder
1 teaspoon sesame oil
1 fresh jalapeño pepper, seeded and
   chopped, or to taste*

4 SERVINGS

1 Cook pasta according to package directions. Drain and rinse
  with cold water; drain again.

2 Wash and peel pineapple. Cut in half and remove eyes and core.
  Cut into bite-sized pieces. Wash and peel papaya; cut in half and
scoop out seeds. Cut into bite-sized pieces.

3 Place cooked, cooled pasta, pineapple, papaya, romaine lettuce,
  and chicken in a large bowl; toss to mix. Divide salad among
four salad plates.

Dressing

1 Stir dressing ingredients in a bowl; drizzle over each salad.
  Serve. Refrigerate leftovers.

*Do not touch your eyes when working with jalapeños!

Serve this curried salad topped with toasted cashew halves.

Sam's Chicken Salad in Fresh Cantaloupe Boats

1 Place chicken, bell pepper, red onion and tarragon in a medium bowl.

2 Whisk olive oil, vinegar, marmalade, mustard and salt in a small bowl; pour over chicken mixture. Toss well until coated. Place equal amounts in each cantaloupe half. Serve slightly chilled along with warm hard rolls. Refrigerate leftovers.

Enjoy this tarragon chicken salad with juicy cantaloupe . . . like Sam, unforgettable.

Variation: Serve chicken salad on a bed of baby spinach with cantaloupe wedges.

INGREDIENTS

3 cups diced rotisserie chicken breast, skin removed
¼ cup minced red bell pepper
2 tablespoons minced red onion
1 tablespoon chopped fresh tarragon
3 tablespoons extra virgin olive oil
3 tablespoons white balsamic vinegar
1½ tablespoons orange marmalade
½ tablespoon Dijon mustard
¼ teaspoon salt
2 cantaloupes, washed, halved and seeds removed

4 SERVINGS

Walnut Curried Chicken Salad

INGREDIENTS

1 boneless, skinless rotisserie chicken
1½ cups mayonnaise
2 to 3 tablespoons curry powder
1 tablespoon ground cumin
1 tablespoon Dijon mustard
½ teaspoon ground black pepper
¼ cup mango chutney
¼ cup chopped flat leaf parsley
4 green onions, white and green
   parts, thinly sliced
3 cups seedless red grapes, halved
1½ cups (6 ounces) chopped
   toasted walnuts
Salt, to taste
Red leaf lettuce

8 SERVINGS

1 Remove skin and meat from chicken and cut into bite-sized pieces.

2 Whisk mayonnaise, curry powder, cumin, mustard, black pepper and chutney in a large bowl. Add parsley, onions, grapes, walnuts and chicken. Stir gently to coat all ingredients. Add more curry powder if needed, and add salt to taste. Serve over red leaf lettuce on individual salad plates. Refrigerate leftovers.

Walnuts and grapes are used in this easy-to-prepare chicken salad.

Serve with warm rolls along with assorted sliced melons.

Chili, Chowder & Stew

Mary Dow's Beef and Chicken Chili

INGREDIENTS

1 tablespoon corn oil
½ pound lean ground beef, seasoned
   with salt and black pepper
1 large yellow onion, chopped
3 cloves garlic, coarsely chopped
½ cup chopped green bell pepper
½ cup thinly sliced celery
1 tablespoon chili powder
1 teaspoon ground cumin
½ teaspoon oregano leaves
2 cups finely diced rotisserie chicken,
   skin removed
1 16-ounce can stewed tomatoes
1 8-ounce can tomato sauce
½ cup water
1 16-ounce pinto beans, drained

4 SERVINGS

1 Heat corn oil in a large skillet over medium-high heat. Add beef; cook and stir until meat is no longer pink; drain all but 1 teaspoon fat. Add onion, garlic, bell pepper and celery; cook and stir 5 minutes.

2 Stir in remaining ingredients except beans. Bring mixture to a boil. Reduce heat to medium-low; cook, partially covered, stirring occasionally, for 15 minutes. Remove cover. Stir in beans; cook 5 minutes. Serve hot. Refrigerate leftovers.

Spoon each serving over hot, cooked long grain white rice on a dinner plate. Serve with a crisp green salad, dressed with Italian dressing, along with crusty bread.

Variation: Serve in bowls topped with sour cream or cottage cheese and chopped green onions along with crisp crackers.

White Chicken Chili

1 Heat corn oil in a large saucepan over medium heat. Add onion; cook and stir until soft but not brown. Add garlic, stir and cook a few seconds. Stir in chopped green chiles, jalapeños, cumin, oregano and cayenne pepper; cook and stir 2 minutes.

2 Stir in broth, chicken and beans; simmer 15 minutes, stirring occasionally. Remove from heat. Stir in cheese until melted. Serve hot, with crackers. Refrigerate leftovers.

This chili is fairly hot . . . serve only to fans of spicy food.

 Tip: Serve over hot, cooked rice along with a green salad.

INGREDIENTS

1 tablespoon corn oil
1 cup chopped yellow onion
4 cloves garlic, minced
1 4-ounce can chopped green chiles
1 tablespoon canned jalapeño peppers, or to taste
2 teaspoons ground cumin
1 teaspoon oregano leaves, crushed
⅛ teaspoon ground cayenne pepper, or to taste
2 14-ounce cans chicken broth
3 cups chopped rotisserie chicken, skin removed
3 15-ounce cans great northern beans, undrained
1 cup Monterey Jack cheese
Crispy crackers

4 SERVINGS

Cheesy Vegetable Chicken Chowder

INGREDIENTS

1 cup small broccoli florets
1 cup frozen whole kernel corn
½ cup water
¼ cup finely chopped onion
1½ teaspoons snipped fresh thyme or
  ½ teaspoon dried thyme, crushed
2 cups whole milk
1½ cups chopped rotisserie chicken,
  skin removed
1 10-ounce can condensed cream of
  potato soup
1 cup shredded Cheddar cheese,
  divided
⅛ teaspoon ground black pepper

4 SERVINGS

1 Bring broccoli, corn, water, onions and thyme to a boil in a large saucepan. Reduce heat. Cover and simmer until vegetables are tender, about 10 minutes. Do not drain.

2 Stir in milk, chicken, potato soup, ¾ cup cheese and black pepper. Cook and stir over medium heat until cheese melts and mixture is heated through. Ladle chowder into individual bowls; sprinkle remaining cheese over each serving. Refrigerate leftovers.

A can of potato soup is used to make this quick chicken chowder. Serve with warm, crusty bread.

Chicken Corn Chowder

1 Heat butter in a large heavy kettle over medium heat. Add onions, celery and jalapeño; cook and stir 3 minutes.

2 Add flour and cook, stirring constantly, for 1 minute. Slowly stir in milk until blended.

3 Stir in remaining ingredients. Bring to a boil. Reduce heat to medium; stir and cook until thickened, about 5 minutes. Serve hot. Refrigerate leftovers.

*Do not touch your eyes when working with jalapeños!

Serve with breadsticks or rolls.

INGREDIENTS

2 tablespoons butter
¼ cup chopped yellow onions
¼ cup chopped celery
¼ fresh jalapeño pepper, seeded and chopped*
2 tablespoons all-purpose flour
3 cups whole milk
2 cups chopped rotisserie chicken breast, skin removed
1½ cups whole kernel corn, fresh or frozen
¼ teaspoon dried thyme
⅛ ground cayenne pepper
⅛ teaspoon salt
1 15-ounce can cream-style corn

6 SERVINGS

Potato Chicken Chowder

INGREDIENTS

3 cup chicken broth
2 cups diced potatoes
1 cup diced celery
1 cup diced carrots
½ cup diced yellow onions
1 teaspoon salt, add more later
   if needed
¼ teaspoon ground black pepper
¼ teaspoon margarine
⅓ cup all-purpose flour
2 cups whole milk
2 cups shredded cheese
2 cups diced rotisserie chicken,
   skin removed

6 SERVINGS

1 Bring chicken broth to a boil in a large saucepan. Add potatoes, celery, carrots, onion, salt and black pepper. Cook uncovered, over medium heat, about 15 minutes or until vegetables are tender.

2 Heat margarine in a another large saucepan over medium-high heat. Stir in flour until blended. Gradually stir in milk until sauce forms; stir mixture into broth mixture.

3 Stir in cheese and chicken; heat thoroughly. Serve hot. Refrigerate leftovers.

Serve with warm, crusty bread.

Black Bean and Sausage Chicken Stew

1 Heat corn oil in a large skillet over medium-high heat. Add onion; cook and stir 5 minutes. Stir in chili powder and cumin; cook 30 seconds.

2 Add remaining ingredients except cheese and cilantro. Reduce heat; simmer 10 minutes, stirring occasionally.

3 Remove from heat. Stir in 1 cup cheese. Ladle stew into bowls; top each serving equally with remaining cheese and cilantro. Serve. Refrigerate leftovers.

Serve with warm bread or crackers.

 Variation: Serve over hot pasta.

INGREDIENTS

- 1 tablespoon corn oil
- 1 medium yellow onion, chopped
- 1 teaspoon chili powder
- 1 teaspoon ground cumin
- 1 14½ ounce can low-sodium chicken broth
- 1 14½ ounce can diced tomatoes with green chiles, undrained
- 1 8-ounce package fully cooked spicy chicken sausage links cut into ½-inch pieces
- 1 cup cubed rotisserie chicken, skin removed
- 1 red bell pepper, diced
- 1 15-ounce can black beans, rinsed and drained
- 1½ cups shredded Mexican 4-cheese blend, divided.
- ¼ cup chopped fresh cilantro

4 SERVINGS

Quick Chicken Stew

INGREDIENTS

4 slices turkey bacon
1 cup diced yellow onion
3 cloves garlic, minced
1 cup diced fresh carrots
½ cup diced red bell pepper
4 cups chicken broth
2 14-ounce cans great northern beans,
  drained and rinsed
3 cups shredded rotisserie chicken,
  skin removed
Salt and black pepper to taste

6 SERVINGS

1 Cook bacon in a large Dutch oven or heavy saucepan until crisp. Remove bacon and drain on paper towels; set aside.

2 Add onion and garlic to bacon fat in same pot. Cook and stir until softened, about 3 minutes. Add carrots and red pepper; cook and stir 3 minutes.

3 Add broth and beans. Bring to a boil, then reduce heat and simmer 15 minutes.

4 Stir in chicken, salt and pepper to taste; cook until heated through. Serve hot, topped with crumbled bacon. Refrigerate leftovers.

Serve with warm, crusty bread.

From the Oven

Baked Chicken Burritos

INGREDIENTS

4 cups skinless shredded rotisserie
chicken
1 cup tomatillo salsa or 1 7-ounce can
salsa verde
2 cups shredded Mexican-style cheese
blend, divided
8 (8-inch) flour tortillas
2 10-ounce containers refrigerated
Alfredo pasta sauce
Shredded iceberg lettuce
Diced avocado

8 SERVINGS

Preheat oven to 375°.

1 Lightly butter a 13x9-inch baking dish

2 Stir chicken, salsa and ½ cup cheese in a large bowl until
combined. Spoon about ½ cup mixture down the middle
of a tortilla. Fold one edge over and roll up. Place, seam down,
in prepared baking dish. Repeat with remaining tortillas and
chicken mixture.

3 Mix pasta sauce and remaining cheese in a bowl; spoon mixture
over burritos.

4 Bake until sauce is bubbling and browned in spots, about
20 minutes. Remove from oven; let stand a few minutes
before serving.

5 Serve topped with lettuce and avocado as desired.
Refrigerate leftovers.

Serve with a side of hot pinto beans and Mexican rice.

Baked Chicken Egg Rolls with Pineapple Dipping Sauce

Preheat oven to 400°.

1 Stir and cook first 8 ingredients in oil in a nonstick skillet over medium heat 5 minutes. Stir in chicken and teriyaki sauce.

2 Moisten edge of wrapper. Place about ⅓ cup of mixture in the center of the wrapper. Fold one corner over the filling; then fold the corners to the left and right of the first corner up and over the filling. Finish by rolling towards the remaining corner. Repeat for remaining egg rolls.

3 Place egg rolls seam-side down on a lightly greased baking sheet; brush egg rolls with corn oil.

4 Bake 20 minutes, turning egg rolls once, or until brown. Serve with dipping sauce as desired. Refrigerate leftovers.

Dipping Sauce

1 Mix pineapple juice, vinegar, brown sugar, soy sauce and white pepper in a saucepan and bring to a boil. Mix cornstarch and cold water in a cup and stir into hot mixture. Cook and stir until thickened. Serve warm. Refrigerate leftovers.

These crispy baked egg rolls are less greasy than deep-fried egg rolls. Serve with chicken chow mein for a complete dinner.

INGREDIENTS

½ cup chopped yellow onions
1 clove garlic, minced
½ cup shredded cabbage
½ cup thinly sliced celery
2 green onions (white and green part), thinly sliced
½ cup fresh bean sprouts
¼ cup shredded carrot
¼ cup water chestnuts, chopped
1 tablespoon sesame oil or canola oil
1 cup chopped rotisserie chicken, skin removed
2 tablespoon spicy ginger teriyaki sauce
6 egg roll wrappers
1 tablespoon corn oil

Dipping Sauce
1½ cups unsweetened pineapple juice
¾ cup cider vinegar
½ cup brown sugar
1 tablespoon soy sauce
⅛ teaspoon white pepper
3 tablespoons cornstarch
2 tablespoons cold water

6 EGG ROLLS

Caesar Chicken Pasta

INGREDIENTS

2 cups (7 ounces) uncooked penne
    pasta
2 cups chopped rotisserie chicken,
    skin removed
¾ cup fat-free creamy Caesar
    salad dressing
½ cup reduced-sodium chicken broth
⅓ cup chopped green onions
¼ cup finely chopped red bell pepper
1½ cups (6 ounces) shredded
    mozzarella cheese
1½ cups Caesar-seasoned croutons

6 SERVINGS

Preheat oven to 350°.

1 Cook pasta according to package directions. Drain.

2 Mix remaining ingredients except croutons in a large bowl. Add cooked pasta; mix well. Spoon mixture into an ungreased 2-quart round baking dish.

3 Top with croutons. Bake until heated through and croutons are golden brown, about 20 minutes. Serve warm. Refrigerate leftovers.

Green salad and warm rolls will round out this delicious quick meal.

Cheesy Chicken Broccoli Calzones

Preheat oven to 350°.

1 Mix soup, cheese, chicken, broccoli, salt and pepper in a large bowl.

2 Separate 16 biscuits and press each into a 6-inch circle. Spoon equal amount of chicken mixture onto the center of each round. Fold dough over filling. Press edges with a fork to seal.

3 Place calzones on a baking sheet coated with nonstick cooking spray. Bake until golden, about 15 minutes. Remove from oven and cool 2 minutes before serving. Refrigerate leftovers.

Serve with a light fruit salad.

INGREDIENTS

1 10-ounce can cream of chicken
  soup, undiluted
2 cups shredded mild Cheddar cheese
1½ cups diced rotisserie chicken
  breast, skin removed
1½ cups frozen chopped broccoli,
  thawed
Salt and black pepper to taste
2 1-pound, 3-ounce packages
  refrigerated golden corn biscuits

16 CALZONES

Cheesy Chicken Tetrazzini

INGREDIENTS

¾ cup boiling water
1 chicken bouillon cube
2½ cups spaghetti, broken into 2-inch
   pieces and cooked according to
   package directions; drained
1 10.75-ounce can cream of
   mushroom soup
1½ cups chopped rotisserie chicken,
   skin removed
1½ cups shredded mild Cheddar
   cheese, divided
½ cup finely chopped yellow onion
1 2-ounce jar chopped pimentos,
   drained
⅛ teaspoon celery salt
⅛ teaspoon freshly ground
   black pepper

6 SERVINGS

Preheat oven to 350°.

1 Stir boiling water and bouillon cube in a large bowl until cube melts.

2 Add cooked spaghetti, soup, chicken, ½ cup cheese, onion, pimentos, celery salt and black pepper; mix well.

3 Spoon mixture into an 8x8-inch baking dish. Top with remaining cheese. Bake about 20 minutes or until bubbly and cheese is melted. Remove from oven. Let stand 5 minutes before serving. Refrigerate leftovers.

Serve with a lettuce and tomato salad with Italian dressing.

Chicken and Cheese Stuffed
Portobello Mushrooms

Preheat oven to 450°.

1 Place mushroom caps stem side up on a nonstick baking sheet.

2 Mix remaining ingredients in a medium bowl until blended; spoon mixture equally into each mushroom.

3 Bake until hot and cheese is melted, about 15 minutes. Serve hot. Refrigerate leftovers.

Serve with a green salad and garlic breadsticks.

INGREDIENTS

4 large portobello mushrooms,
   cleaned and stems removed
2 cups chopped rotisserie chicken,
   skin removed
1 ½ cups shredded Italian blend cheese
½ cup finely chopped green
   onion tops
¼ cup sun-dried tomato spread
2 teaspoons Italian seasoning

4 SERVINGS

Chicken and Ham Cheese Quiches

INGREDIENTS

1 purchased refrigerated pie crust
8 eggs
¼ teaspoon salt
¼ teaspoon ground black pepper
⅔ cup whole milk
1 cup shredded Cheddar cheese
½ cup chopped rotisserie chicken,
    skin removed
½ cup chopped fully cooked ham

6 SERVINGS

Preheat oven to 375°.

1 Lightly spray 6 large muffin cups with cooking spray.

2 Cut six 3½-inch circles from pie crust; press into bottoms of prepared muffin cups.

3 Beat eggs, salt, pepper and milk in a medium bowl. Stir in cheese, chicken and ham. Fill prepared muffin cups equally with mixture.

4 Bake until puffed and lightly browned, about 20 minutes. Cool slightly; remove from muffin cups. Serve hot. Refrigerate leftovers.

Serve these little quiches with a leafy green salad and slices of fresh melon.

Chicken and Noodle Casserole

Preheat oven to 400°.

1 Stir all ingredients except shredded Cheddar cheese in a 1½-quart baking dish. Bake about 20 minutes or until hot. Stir.

2 Top with Cheddar cheese. Serve immediately. Refrigerate leftovers.

Serve with a green salad or a side of green beans.

1 10-ounce can condensed cream of mushroom soup, heated

½ cup whole milk, heated

2 cups cubed rotisserie chicken, skin removed

2 cups medium egg noodles, cooked according to package directions; drained

¼ cup grated Parmesan cheese

¼ teaspoon ground black pepper

½ cup shredded Cheddar cheese

4 SERVINGS

Chicken and Stuffing Casserole

INGREDIENTS

1 8-ounce package bread stuffing mix
4 tablespoons butter or margarine,
  melted
1 10-ounce can cream of chicken soup
1 10-ounce can cream of celery soup
1 cup evaporated milk
1 cup chicken broth
2 cups diced rotisserie chicken,
  skin removed
1½ cups frozen peas
2 stalks celery, chopped
½ cup chopped yellow onion
Salt and black pepper to taste

4 SERVINGS

Preheat oven to 350°.

1 Grease a 13x9x2-inch baking dish.

2 Mix stuffing and margarine in a medium bowl; divide in half. Line bottom of a prepared baking dish with half the mixture.

3 Heat soups, milk and broth in a large saucepan until just warm. Place in a large bowl. Add chicken, peas, celery, onion, salt and pepper; mix well. Spread mixture over the stuffing in baking dish.

4 Spread the remaining half of the stuffing on top and gently pat down. Bake about 20 minutes or until hot and bubbly and vegetables are done.

Serve with warm rolls and a lettuce and tomato salad with Italian dressing.

Chicken, Broccoli and Rice Casserole

Preheat oven to 350°.

1 Lightly butter a 2½-quart baking dish.

2 Mix stuffing and margarine in a medium bowl; divide in half. Line bottom of a prepared baking dish with half the mixture.

3 Mix soup and sour cream in a large bowl until blended. Add remaining ingredients except French fried onions; mix well. Pour mixture into prepared baking dish.

4 Bake until hot and bubbly, about 20 minutes, topping with onions for the last 2 minutes. Serve hot. Refrigerate leftovers.

Serve with a side of fresh sliced tomatoes and warm rolls.

INGREDIENTS

1 10-ounce can Cheddar cheese soup
½ cup sour cream
2 cups cubed rotisserie chicken breast, skin removed
1 cup cooked long grain white rice
1 16-ounce package frozen chopped broccoli, cooked and drained
¼ teaspoon salt
¼ teaspoon ground black pepper
1⅓ cups French fried onions

4 SERVINGS

Chicken, Chile and Cheese Stuffed Potatoes

INGREDIENTS

2 large russet potatoes, scrubbed
⅓ cup light sour cream
2 teaspoons Mexican blend seasoning
1 cup shredded rotisserie chicken,
  skin removed
1 cup shredded Mexican blend cheese
2 tablespoons each diced vegetables,
  red bell pepper, celery, onion
  and tomato
1 4-ounce can diced green chiles
½ teaspoon diced, seeded fresh
  jalapeño pepper, or to taste*

2 SERVINGS

1 Place potatoes on a microwave-safe plate. Pierce skin of potatoes in several places with a fork. Cover tightly with plastic wrap. Pierce plastic with a small knife to vent; microwave on high for 10 minutes, or until potatoes are cooked through. Let cool slightly, then cut in half lengthwise; scoop out potato pulp into a medium bowl, leaving a ½-inch shell of pulp inside the skin.

2 Place potato skins in a shallow microwave-safe baking dish; set aside.

3 Mash potato pulp with a fork. Stir in sour cream and Mexican seasoning. Add remaining ingredients, stirring mixture just until combined.

4 Spoon mixture into potato shells; cover with plastic wrap and microwave on high for 5 minutes. Serve hot. Refrigerate leftovers.

*Do not touch your eyes when working with jalapeños!

Serve with a crisp green salad.

Variation: Use canned, sliced jalapeños instead of green chiles for more spice!

Chicken Enchiladas

Preheat oven to 375°.

1 Heat oil in a medium skillet. Add onion and garlic; cook and stir until softened, about 1 minute; place in a large bowl. Add chicken, 2 cups cheese, chiles, olives and ¾ cup enchilada sauce; mix well.

2 Heat tortillas in a skillet or microwave until soft, according to package directions.

3 Pour a small amount of enchilada sauce in the bottom of two 13x9-inch baking pans, just enough to cover the bottom. Dip each tortilla in enchilada sauce. Place about ⅓ cup chicken mixture across the middle of each tortilla and roll up. Place tortillas seam side down in prepared pans. Pour remaining enchilada sauce over the top.

4 Cover loosely with aluminum foil and bake 20 minutes. Remove foil; top with remaining cheese. Continue baking, uncovered, until cheese melts. Serve hot. Refrigerate leftovers.

Serve topped with sour cream and sliced green onions, as desired.

INGREDIENTS

- 1 tablespoon corn oil
- 1 medium onion, chopped
- 2 cloves garlic, minced
- 2 shredded rotisserie chicken breasts, skin removed
- 4 cups shredded cheese (pepper jack, Cheddar, or a mixture), divided
- 1 4-ounce can diced green chiles
- 1 2-ounce can sliced ripe olives, drained
- 4 10-ounce cans enchilada sauce, divided
- 12 corn tortillas

12 ENCHILADAS

Chicken Tostadas

INGREDIENTS

4 (6-inch) corn tortillas
1 16-ounce can fat free refried beans
1¾ cups chopped rotisserie chicken
  (skin removed), mixed with
  1 teaspoon cumin
1 ripe avocado, peeled, pitted and
  sliced into wedges
2 cups shredded reduced fat Mexican
  4-cheese blend, divided
1½ cups thinly sliced romaine lettuce
1 cup chopped fresh tomato
¾ cup chunky-style salsa

4 SERVINGS

Preheat oven to 400°.

1 Spray both sides of tortillas with no-stick cooking spray. Place on a baking sheet; bake 10 minutes or until golden brown and crisp. Place on four serving plates.

2 Heat beans and rotisserie chicken separately, in the microwave or in small pots on the stove, until hot throughout.

3 Spread each tortilla with beans, then top with avocado slices, chicken, cheese, lettuce, tomato and salsa. Serve immediately. Refrigerate leftovers.

Serve this quick-to-fix meal with grapes and wedges of fresh melon.

Variation: Use pepper jack cheese.

Creamy Broccoli Chicken Pasta Bake

Preheat oven to 450°.

1 Cook pasta according to package directions; add broccoli to water 1 minute before pasta is done. Drain; place in an 11x7-inch baking dish.

2 Stir in soup and chicken. Top with cheese. Bake about 10 minutes or until cheese is melted and mixture is hot and bubbly. Refrigerate leftovers.

Serve with warm hard rolls.

INGREDIENTS

8 ounces uncooked penne pasta
1½ cups small broccoli florets
1 25-ounce container three cheese
  and broccoli soup, heated
1½ cups shredded rotisserie chicken
¼ cup shredded Parmesan cheese

6 SERVINGS

Creamy Chicken Bean Enchiladas

INGREDIENTS

2 3-ounce packages cream cheese
1 cup mild chunky salsa
2 cups shredded Colby Jack cheese or
    Mexican cheese, divided
2 cups shredded rotisserie chicken
    breast, skin removed
1 15-ounce can pinto beans, drained
6 (6-inch) flour tortillas

6 SERVINGS

Preheat oven to 350°.

1 Lightly butter a 13x9-inch glass baking dish.

2 Stir cream cheese, salsa and 1 cup Colby Jack cheese in a sauce-pan over medium heat, stirring constantly, until cheese is melted and well blended.

3 Remove from heat. Stir in chicken and beans.

4 Place equal amounts of mixture across the center of each tortilla. Roll and place seam-side down into prepared baking dish. Cover with aluminum foil.

5 Bake about 20 minutes or until heated through. Remove foil. Top with remaining cheese and continue baking, uncovered, until cheese is melted. Serve warm. Refrigerate leftovers.

This creamy delight is so easy to prepare. Serve over a bed of shredded lettuce along with a side of sliced fresh tomatoes, avocados and sour cream.

Variations: Use black beans instead of pinto beans. Use enchilada sauce instead of salsa.

Corn Tortilla Chicken Bake

Preheat oven to 400°.

1 Lightly butter a 2-quart shallow baking dish.

2 Mix soup, salsa, milk, chicken, tortillas and half the cheese in a large bowl. Pour mixture into prepared baking dish.

3 Cover baking dish and bake about 20 minutes or until mixture is hot and bubbling. Remove from oven; sprinkle with cheese and let stand until cheese is melted. Serve. Refrigerate leftovers.

Serve with buttered green beans or a crisp green salad and warm rolls.

INGREDIENTS

1 10.75-ounce can condensed tomato soup, heated
1 cup chunky salsa, heated
½ cup whole milk, heated
2 cups cubed rotisserie chicken, skin removed
8 (6-inch) corn tortillas cut into 1-inch pieces
1 cup shredded Cheddar cheese, divided

4 SERVINGS

Croissant Chicken Bake

INGREDIENTS

2 8-ounce containers refrigerated
  crescent rolls
2 cups shredded rotisserie chicken,
  skin removed
1 10.75-ounce can condensed cream
  of celery soup
1 10.75-ounce can condensed cream
  of chicken soup
1 8-ounce container sour cream
1 cup chicken stock

4 SERVINGS

Preheat oven to 350°.

1 Spray a 3-quart shallow baking dish with cooking spray.

2 Separate dough into 15 triangles. Spoon ¼ cup chicken onto each triangle. Roll up triangles around chicken. Place rolls in prepared baking dish.

3 Stir soups, sour cream and stock in a medium bowl. Pour mixture over rolls.

4 Bake about 20 minutes or until rolls are golden brown. Serve. Refrigerate leftovers.

This is a nice dish to serve for brunch. Serve with a fresh fruit salad.

Enchilada Bake

Preheat oven to 450°.

1 Pour half of 1 can of tomato sauce into the bottom of an 11x7-inch microwave-safe baking dish. Layer with half of tortillas, chiles and chicken and ⅓ cup cheese. Pour the other half of the first can of tomato sauce over the top, then repeat another layer with the remaining half of tortillas, chiles and chicken, and ⅓ cup cheese.

2 Pour remaining can of tomato sauce over the top and sprinkle with remaining cheese.

3 Cover with plastic wrap; microwave on high for 10 minutes. Remove plastic wrap. Cover loosely with aluminum foil and bake for 10 minutes. Serve hot. Top with green onions, avocado and sour cream, as desired, when serving. Refrigerate leftovers.

A side of flavored rice and pinto beans will add to this meal.

INGREDIENTS

2 7.5-ounce cans Mexican-style tomato sauce, divided
6 (6-inch) corn tortillas, cut into 1-inch strips, divided
1 4-ounce can diced green chiles, divided
2 cups shredded rotisserie chicken, skin removed
1 cup shredded Mexican blend cheese, divided
Sliced green onions
Avocado slices
Sour cream

6 SERVINGS

Greek Chicken Casserole

INGREDIENTS

1 10.75-ounce can condensed cream of chicken soup
½ cup chicken broth
4 cups chopped rotisserie chicken, skin discarded
4 cups ½-inch pieces fresh zucchini
½ cup chopped red onion
1½ teaspoons Greek seasoning, divided
2 cloves garlic, minced
2 6-inch pita bread rounds, cut into bite-sized wedges
Nonstick cooking spray
1 cup chopped fresh Roma tomatoes
1 cup (4 ounces) crumbled feta cheese
½ cup pitted Kalamata olives, sliced

4 SERVINGS

Preheat oven to 350°.

1 Heat soup and chicken broth in a small saucepan.

2 Stir soup mixture, chicken, zucchini, onion, 1 teaspoon Greek seasoning and garlic in a large bowl. Pour mixture into an ungreased 3-quart glass baking dish.

3 Cut pita breads into bite-sized wedges. Coat wedges with cooking spray and sprinkle with remaining Greek seasoning; sprinkle wedges evenly over chicken mixture. Sprinkle evenly with tomatoes, cheese and olives.

3 Bake uncovered until thoroughly heated, about 20 minutes. Serve hot. Refrigerate any leftovers.

Zucchini and Greek-seasoned pita bread star in this tasty casserole.

Green Chile Chicken Enchiladas

Preheat oven to 375°.

1 Coat a 13x9-inch baking dish with cooking spray.

2 Mix 1½ cups cheese, chicken, artichokes, chiles, onion and 2 tablespoons enchilada sauce in a medium bowl.

3 Soften tortillas according to package directions. Fill each tortilla with about ¼ cup cheese mixture; roll up and place seam-side down in prepared baking dish. Pour remaining enchilada sauce over filled tortillas; sprinkle with remaining cheese.

4 Bake about 20 minutes or until cheese is melted and filling is hot. Remove from oven; sprinkle with tomatoes. Serve immediately, topped with sour cream. Refrigerate leftovers.

A side of fresh fruit or sliced melon will complement this dish.

INGREDIENTS

2 cups shredded Mexican 4-cheese blend, divided
1 cup shredded rotisserie chicken, skin removed
½ cup artichoke hearts
1 4.5-ounce can chopped green chiles, undrained
2 green onions, sliced
1 10-ounce can green enchilada sauce, divided
8 (6-inch) flour tortillas
1 large fresh tomato, chopped
Sour cream

4 SERVINGS

Oven Chow Mein Chicken

INGREDIENTS

¼ cup butter or margarine
1 medium yellow onion, chopped
3 stalks celery, chopped
1 10.75-ounce can condensed cream
   of mushroom soup
½ cup chicken broth
1 tablespoon soy sauce
3 cups cubed rotisserie chicken,
   skin removed
½ cup sliced fresh mushrooms
1 3-ounce can chow mein noodles
⅓ cup salted cashew halves

4 SERVINGS

Preheat oven to 350°.

1 Heat butter in a large saucepan. Add onions and celery; cook and stir until tender.

2 Stir in soup, broth and soy sauce. Add chicken and mushrooms; cook until heated.

3 Place mixture in a greased 2-quart baking dish. Sprinkle top with noodles and nuts. Bake uncovered until heated, about 15 minutes.

This tasty dish is fresh from the oven . . . forget take-out!

Quick Chicken Casserole

Preheat oven to 400°.

1 Lightly butter a 2-quart baking dish.

2 Mix soup, milk, cheese, garlic powder, and black pepper in a large bowl.

3 Stir in cooked elbow macaroni, chicken and cooked peas and carrots. Pour mixture into prepared baking dish.

4 Bake 20 minutes, then stir. Crush stuffing mix and mix in a bowl with Parmesan cheese and butter; sprinkle evenly over casserole. Continue baking until piping hot. Refrigerate leftovers.

Serve with a garden salad and warm rolls.

INGREDIENTS

1 10.75-ounce can condensed cream of broccoli soup
1 cup whole milk
½ cup shredded mozzarella cheese
¼ teaspoon garlic powder
⅛ teaspoon ground black pepper
2 cups hot, cooked elbow macaroni
2 cups cubed rotisserie chicken, skin removed
1 10-ounce package frozen peas and carrots, cooked and drained
½ cup herb-seasoned stuffing mix
2 tablespoon grated Parmesan cheese
2 tablespoons butter or margarine, melted

8 SERVINGS

Scalloped Chicken and Pasta Casserole

INGREDIENTS

2¼ cups cold water
¼ cup margarine or butter, divided
1 6.2-ounce package pasta shells and
   white cheddar mix
2 cups frozen mixed vegetables
⅔ cup whole milk
2 cups chopped rotisserie chicken,
   skin removed
¼ cup dried bread crumbs

4 SERVINGS

Preheat oven to 450°.

1 Bring water and 2 tablespoons margarine to a boil in a 3-quart saucepan. Stir in pasta (reserve seasoning packet) and frozen vegetables. Reduce heat to medium and boil, uncovered, stirring frequently, about 12 minutes or until most of the water is absorbed.

2 Add contents of seasoning packet, milk and chicken; cook 3 minutes. Place mixture in a lightly buttered 8- or 9-inch glass baking dish.

3 Melt remaining 2 tablespoons margarine in a small saucepan; stir in dried bread crumbs. Sprinkle over pasta mixture. Bake until edges are bubbly and bread crumbs are browned. Serve hot. Refrigerate leftovers.

This is an easy supper to prepare. Serve with a green salad and soft rolls.

Tamale Chicken Casserole

Preheat oven to 350°.

1 Lightly butter an 8x8-inch baking dish. Sprinkle crushed corn chips evenly onto bottom of prepared baking dish. Unwrap tamales; layer over corn chips.

2 Mix chili, chicken, corn and chiles in a large bowl. Spoon mixture evenly over tamales.

3 Bake 20 minutes. Sprinkle with cheese; bake until melted. Serve hot, topped as desired, with sour cream. Refrigerate leftovers.

Serve with a side of flavored rice, along with sliced fresh cantaloupe.

INGREDIENTS

1 cup finely crushed corn chips
1 15-ounce can tamales
1 10-ounce can chili
1½ cups chopped rotisserie chicken, skin removed
1 8-ounce can whole kernel corn, undrained
1 4-ounce can chopped green chiles, drained
1 cup shredded Cheddar cheese
Sour cream

4 SERVINGS

Upside-Down Chicken Pot Pie

INGREDIENTS

1 7.5-ounce container refrigerated
  flaky buttermilk biscuits
1 10-ounce package frozen mixed
  vegetables, thawed
1½ cups water
½ cup whole milk
1 package chicken-flavored pasta
  side dish mix
2 cups cut-up rotisserie chicken,
  skin removed
1½ cups shredded Cheddar cheese,
  divided

6 SERVINGS

Preheat oven to 450°.

1 Spray a deep-dish pie pan with nonstick cooking spray.

2 Pull biscuits apart and press onto bottom and up sides of prepared pie pan. Press edges of biscuits together to make a crust. Bake 8 minutes or until golden; remove from oven and set aside.

3 Bring vegetables, water and milk to a boil in a medium saucepan over high heat. Stir in pasta side dish mix. Return to a boil over high heat. Reduce heat to medium and cook, covered, stirring occasionally, 8 minutes or until pasta is tender.

4 Stir in chicken and 1 cup cheese. Spoon mixture into prepared pie pan. Sprinkle with remaining cheese.

5 Bake uncovered for 10 minutes or until cheese is melted. Serve hot. Refrigerate leftovers.

Serve this cozy pie with wedges of fresh cantaloupe.

Stove-Top Main
Dishes with Pasta

Angel Hair Pasta with Lemon and Chicken

INGREDIENTS

1 9-ounce package refrigerated angel
hair pasta
1½ cups diced rotisserie chicken
2 tablespoons extra virgin olive oil
1 tablespoon butter, melted
2 to 3 tablespoons fresh lemon juice
2 tablespoons chopped fresh parsley
¼ teaspoon marjoram
¼ teaspoon garlic powder
Salt and ground black pepper to taste
Parmesan cheese

4 SERVINGS

1 Prepare pasta according to package directions.

2 Toss pasta with chicken, olive oil, butter, lemon juice, parsley, marjoram and garlic powder in a large bowl. Season with salt and black pepper to taste.

3 Top with a generous amount of Parmesan cheese and serve. Refrigerate leftovers.

Serve this quick main dish with a tossed green salad.

Angel Hair Pasta with Shrimp and Chicken

1 Heat olive oil in a medium-sized nonstick skillet. Add onion; cook and stir over medium heat until very soft.

2 Add shrimp, bell pepper, garlic, oregano and salt. Cook and stir until shrimp are pink, about 5 to 8 minutes.

3 Add chicken, tomatoes and lemon juice; stir and cook until thoroughly heated. Season with black pepper to taste. Serve immediately over hot pasta. Refrigerate leftovers.

Serve a green salad and crusty bread to complete this tasty meal.

INGREDIENTS

1 tablespoon extra virgin olive oil
½ cup chopped yellow onion
1 pound fresh shrimp, peeled and deveined
½ cup chopped green bell pepper
3 cloves garlic, finely chopped
1 teaspoon dried oregano leaves
¼ teaspoon salt
1½ cups finely cubed rotisserie chicken breast, skin removed
3 fresh, ripe tomatoes, cored and chopped
1 tablespoon fresh lemon juice
Ground black pepper to taste
6 ounces angel hair pasta, cooked according to package directions

4 SERVINGS

Asparagus and Pancetta Chicken Pasta Toss

INGREDIENTS

8 ounces uncooked rotelle or
   penne pasta
1 cup fresh asparagus cut diagonally
   into 1-inch pieces
½ cup chopped pancetta
1 cup chopped yellow onion
1 clove garlic, minced
1 tablespoon olive oil
1 small red bell pepper, cut into strips
½ teaspoon salt
¼ teaspoon ground black pepper
2 cups cubed rotisserie chicken breast,
   skin removed
¾ cup half-and-half
1 cup shredded Italian 6-cheese blend
2 tablespoons chopped fresh basil
3 tablespoons shredded Parmesan
   cheese

4 SERVINGS

1 Cook pasta according to package directions; drain and keep warm.

2 Place asparagus and 1 tablespoon water in a microwave-safe bowl; cover and microwave on high 3 minutes or until asparagus is crisp-tender. Rinse with cool water; drain and set aside.

3 Cook pancetta in a large skillet until slightly brown. Add onion and garlic; cook and stir 5 minutes. Add olive oil, bell pepper, salt and pepper; cook and stir 5 minutes. Add chicken; cook and stir 2 minutes.

4 Add half-and-half and cooked asparagus; cook over medium heat for 2 minutes, or until asparagus is heated through. Stir in Italian cheese until melted.

5 Toss warm cooked pasta with chicken mixture and basil. Serve on individual salad plates. Top each with Parmesan cheese. Serve immediately. Refrigerate leftovers.

Serve with warm, crusty rolls and green salad.

Variation: Use cooked bacon instead of pancetta.

Asparagus Chicken and Prosciutto Pasta Skillet

1 Cook pasta according to package directions; drain.

2 Heat olive oil in a large skillet over medium heat. Add onion and prosciutto; stir and cook until onions start to brown, about 8 minutes.

3 Add chicken; cook and stir 2 minutes. Add asparagus; cook and stir 5 minutes. Add tomatoes. Cover and cook 5 minutes. Remove cover. Stir in water. Cook until liquid has evaporated. Remove from heat. Add pasta and toss. Add cheese and toss again. Season with salt and pepper to taste. Serve immediately. Refrigerate leftovers.

Serve with Italian bread.

INGREDIENTS

16 ounce package uncooked fusilli or penne pasta
1 tablespoon olive oil
1 medium yellow onion, cut in half and thinly sliced
¼ pound thinly sliced prosciutto, cut into thin strips
1 cup cubed rotisserie chicken breast, skin removed
1 pound tender asparagus, trimmed and cut diagonally into 1-inch pieces
2 cups halved cherry tomatoes
¼ cup cold water
½ cup grated Pecorino Romano cheese
Salt and black pepper to taste

6 SERVINGS

Bacon and Chicken Spaghetti with Tomato Sauce

INGREDIENTS

1 8-ounce package spaghetti
3 leeks, roots and rough tops trimmed
2 tablespoon olive oil
6 slices bacon cut into thin pieces
3 cloves garlic, minced
1½ cups diced rotisserie chicken,
  skin removed
1 28-ounce can Italian whole tomatoes
  in puree, undrained
¼ cup fresh flat leaf parsley
Salt and black pepper to taste

4 SERVINGS

1 Cook spaghetti according to package directions. Drain; reserve ½ cup pasta water.

2 Cut the leeks in half lengthwise and then slice thinly. Wash slices in cold water to remove dirt. Dry on clean kitchen towel.

3 Heat olive oil in a large, deep skillet. Add bacon; cook until crisp. Stir in leeks and garlic; cook abut 2 minutes or until softened. Stir in chicken; cook and stir 2 minutes. Add tomatoes; crush tomatoes with potato masher. Stir in flat leaf parsley. Bring mixture to a boil, then immediately lower heat; simmer 10 minutes. Season with salt and pepper to taste. Add cooked spaghetti and pasta water. Toss mixture a few minutes to coat thoroughly. Serve hot. Refrigerate leftovers.

Top with freshly grated Parmesan cheese and torn fresh basil when serving. Serve with warm French bread . . . buttered of course.

Chicken and Red Pepper Pasta

1 Cook fettuccine according to package directions. Drain.

2 Process red peppers and chiles in a blender or food processor until smooth (add a small amount of cold water if mixture is too thick); set sauce aside.

3 Coat a large nonstick skillet with cooking spray. Add garlic; cook, stirring constantly, for 30 seconds over medium-high heat. Add chicken; cook and stir until warm.

4 Stir in fettuccine, pepper sauce, rehydrated tomatoes and green onions. Cook and stir 5 minutes or until heated through. Remove from heat. Stir in 1½ cups cheese. Serve warm; top each serving equally with remaining cheese. Refrigerate leftovers.

Serve this zesty pasta dish with a crisp lettuce salad and warm rolls.

INGREDIENTS

1 8-ounce package fettuccine noodles
½ cup roasted red peppers, drained
1 4-ounce can mild green chiles, drained
3 cloves garlic, minced
2 rotisserie chicken breasts, bones and skin removed, cut into 1-inch cubes
½ cup sun-dried tomatoes, rehydrated and chopped
½ cup sliced green onions
2 cups shredded reduced fat Italian 4-cheese blend, divided

4 SERVINGS

Chicken Alfredo with Fettuccine

INGREDIENTS

8 ounces fettuccine
1 tablespoon butter
1½ cups cubed rotisserie chicken
    breast, skin removed
1 clove garlic, finely chopped
1 16-ounce jar Alfredo sauce
Parmesan cheese
Chopped fresh parsley

4 SERVINGS

1 Cook pasta according to package directions. Drain and keep warm.

2 Heat butter in a 12-inch skillet over medium-high heat. Add chicken; stir until heated through, about 2 minutes. Add garlic; cook and stir 1 minute. Stir in Alfredo sauce. Simmer, covered, over low heat, stirring occasionally, for 5 minutes or until heated through.

3 Serve immediately over fettuccine. Sprinkle each serving with Parmesan cheese and garnish with parsley as desired. Refrigerate leftovers.

Serve with a green salad and warm rolls.

Chicken Cacciatore

1 Heat olive oil in a large nonstick skillet. Add chopped onion; cook and stir over medium heat for 5 minutes. Add chicken; stir and cook 2 minutes.

2 Stir in remaining ingredients. Cover and simmer over low heat for 10 minutes.

Serve over angel hair pasta along with warm garlic bread. Add a side of steamed broccoli, topped with Parmesan cheese.

INGREDIENTS

1 tablespoon olive oil
1 cup chopped yellow onion
3 cups skinless rotisserie chicken breast cut into 1-inch pieces
1 16-ounce jar basil-and-tomato marinara sauce
1 14-ounce can mushrooms, drained
1 teaspoon chopped garlic
Salt and black pepper to taste

4 SERVINGS

Chicken Lo Mein

INGREDIENTS

2 packages chicken-flavored ramen
   noodle soup mix
3 cups boiling water
2 tablespoons cornstarch
2 cups chicken broth
2 tablespoons olive oil
1 red bell pepper, sliced
1 yellow bell pepper, sliced
3 cloves garlic, minced
3 green onions, sliced
2 cups snow peas, ends snipped
2 cups sliced mushrooms
2 rotisserie chicken breasts, skin removed, thinly sliced into strips
2 tablespoons low-sodium soy sauce

6 SERVINGS

1 Break noodles into a large bowl. Sprinkle with seasoning packet. Cover with boiling water; set aside. Stir cornstarch into chicken broth in a small bowl; set aside.

2 Heat olive oil in a large, heavy skillet or wok. Stir and cook bell peppers, garlic, green onions, snow peas and mushrooms over medium heat until crisp-tender. Add sliced chicken; stir and cook 2 minutes. Stir in broth mixture; bring to a boil. Stir in soy sauce.

3 Drain noodles and add to skillet mixture. Stir and cook until heated through and sauce is thickened. Serve. Refrigerate leftovers.

Ramen noodle soup is used in this flavorful chicken dish.

Chicken Stroganoff

1 Heat butter and corn oil in a large nonstick skillet. Add onion and mushrooms; cook and stir over medium-high heat to brown vegetables, about 5 minutes. Add chicken; stir and cook 2 minutes.

2 Stir in gravy and dill; simmer, covered, for 10 minutes. Add sour cream and cook until hot. Season to taste with salt and pepper. Stir chicken mixture into hot, cooked noodles. Serve. Refrigerate leftovers.

Serve with a green salad and warm bread.

INGREDIENTS

1 tablespoon butter
1 tablespoon corn oil
1 quartered and sliced yellow onion
1 8-ounce package sliced fresh
    mushrooms
2 cups bite-sized rotisserie chicken
    breast strips
1 12-ounce jar chicken gravy
1 teaspoon chopped fresh dill, or
    ½ teaspoon dried
¾ cup light sour cream
Salt and black pepper to taste
½ pound egg noodles, cooked
    according to directions and kept hot

4 SERVINGS

Chinese Chicken Stir-Fry

INGREDIENTS

1 6-ounce package rice noodles
2 teaspoons corn oil
2 rotisserie chicken breast halves, bones and skin removed, cut into bite-sized strips
1 (9-ounce) package frozen cut broccoli, thawed and drained
2 cups fresh bean sprouts
1 8-ounce can bamboo shoots, drained
½ cup water
2 tablespoons soy sauce
4 teaspoons cornstarch
1 teaspoon granulated sugar
½ teaspoon chicken bouillon

4 SERVINGS

1 Cook rice noodles according to package directions; drain and keep warm.

2 Heat corn oil in a large nonstick skillet over medium-high heat. Add chicken; cook and stir 1 minute. Add broccoli, bean sprouts and bamboo shoots; cook and stir until broccoli is crisp-tender, about 4 minutes.

3 Stir water, soy sauce, cornstarch, sugar and bouillon in a small bowl until blended. Gradually add mixture to chicken mixture, stirring constantly, until thick and bubbly. Serve immediately over cooked rice noodles. Refrigerate leftovers.

Complete this meal with a side of purchased egg rolls . . . and fortune cookies!

Creamy Broccoli and Chicken Pasta

1 Cook noodles according to package directions; drain and keep warm.

2 Melt margarine in a large skillet over medium-high heat. Add broccoli, mushrooms, onion and bell pepper; cook and stir

3 minutes or until vegetables are crisp-tender. Add chicken and broth. Reduce heat and simmer 5 minutes.

4 Mix yogurt, mustard and flour in a small bowl; stir into skillet mixture. Bring to a boil, stirring constantly. Reduce heat to low. Stir in apple juice, salt and pepper; cook until heated through. Spoon mixture over noodles placed on a serving platter. Serve immediately. Refrigerate leftovers.

This delicious entrée is quick to prepare. Serve with a side of sliced fresh tomatoes and warm rolls.

INGREDIENTS

8 ounces no-yolk egg noodles
2 tablespoons margarine
4 cups (8 ounces) broccoli florets
½ pound fresh mushrooms, sliced
½ cup chopped onion
1 small red bell pepper, cut into thin strips
2 boneless, skinless rotisserie chicken breasts, cubed
¾ cup chicken broth
1 8-ounce carton low-fat plain yogurt
1 tablespoon Dijon mustard
3 tablespoons flour
2 tablespoons unsweetened apple juice
½ teaspoon salt
¼ teaspoon pepper

4 SERVINGS

Creamy Chicken and Peas with Noodles

INGREDIENTS

1 10-ounce package medium egg
  noodles
1 tablespoon butter or margarine
½ cup sliced green onions
2 cups frozen peas, thawed
1 8-ounce container garden-vegetable
  cream cheese spread
1¼ cups whole milk
1½ cups chopped rotisserie chicken,
  skin removed
½ teaspoon garlic salt
¼ teaspoon black pepper

4 SERVINGS

1 Cook noodles according to package directions; drain and
keep warm.

2 Heat butter in a 12-inch nonstick skillet over medium heat. Add
onions and peas; cook and stir until onions are crisp-tender,
about 3 minutes. Add cream cheese and milk; stir until well blended. Stir in chicken, garlic salt and black pepper; cook until hot.

3 Stir noodles into chicken mixture; cook until heated through.
Serve hot. Refrigerate leftovers.

Serve with fresh cucumber and tomato slices.

Variation: Use your favorite vegetable instead of peas.

Creamy Chicken Breasts with Angel Hair Pasta

1 Cook angel hair pasta according to package directions; drain and keep warm.

2 Melt butter in a saucepan over low heat. Add garlic; cook and stir 1 minute. Add sun-dried tomatoes and ¾ cup chicken broth. Bring to a boil over medium heat, then reduce heat and simmer 10 minutes. Add cream; bring to a boil, stirring constantly. Reduce heat; simmer over medium heat until thickened.

3 While sauce is cooking, heat olive oil in a large nonstick skillet over medium heat. Add chicken; cook, turning once, until heated through. Remove from skillet; keep warm.

4 Drain all but 1 tablespoon drippings from skillet. Add remaining ¼ cup chicken broth to skillet; bring to a boil. Stir in basil. Add mixture to cream sauce.

5 Place chicken over warm pasta. Top evenly with warm sauce and serve immediately. Refrigerate leftovers.

Serve with a crisp green salad and garlic breadsticks.

INGREDIENTS

8 ounces angel hair pasta
1 tablespoon butter
2 cloves garlic, minced
½ cup sun-dried tomatoes, chopped
1 cup chicken broth, divided
1 cup heavy cream
2 tablespoons olive oil
4 rotisserie chicken breast halves, bones and skin removed, cut up and seasoned with ½ teaspoon black pepper or to taste
2 tablespoons chopped fresh basil

4 SERVINGS

Creamy Chicken Cheese Skillet

INGREDIENTS

8 ounces uncooked whole wheat
  penne pasta
2 cups cauliflower cut into
  ½-inch pieces
1½ tablespoons olive oil
1 small yellow onion, finely chopped
½ cup chicken broth
3 cups whole milk
3 tablespoons all-purpose flour
½ teaspoon salt, or to taste
½ teaspoon ground black pepper
1 cup shredded Swiss cheese
3 cups shredded rotisserie chicken,
  skin removed
1 teaspoon Dijon mustard
2 tablespoons chopped green onions

6 SERVINGS

1 Cook pasta in a large pot, according to package directions, and add cauliflower to the pot for the last 5 minutes of cooking time. Drain; keep in pot.

2 Heat olive oil in a large skillet over medium heat. Add onion; cook and stir until tender, about 2 minutes. Add broth; cook 3 minutes.

3 Whisk milk, flour, salt and pepper in a medium bowl until well blended; stir into skillet. Bring to a boil over medium heat, stirring constantly, until thickened, about 2 minutes.

4 Reduce heat to low. Stir in cheese until smooth. Stir in chicken and mustard; cook until heated through. Stir mixture into the cooked pasta and cauliflower. Sprinkle with chopped green onions. Serve. Refrigerate leftovers.

Serve this easy, cheesy meal with a green salad.

 Variation: Use other pasta.

Dill and Feta Chicken Pasta

1 Cook pasta according to package directions; drain and keep hot.

2 Mix tomatoes, green onions, dill, flat leaf parsley, olive oil and pepper in a large bowl.

3 Add chicken, feta and pasta; season with salt to taste. Toss and serve. Refrigerate leftovers.

Serve with a crisp green salad and warm Italian bread.

INGREDIENTS

16 ounces penne pasta
4 cups coarsely chopped ripe
  tomatoes
1 cup chopped green onions
⅓ cup chopped fresh dill
¼ cup chopped flat leaf parsley
⅓ cup extra virgin olive oil
½ teaspoon freshly ground pepper
2 rotisserie chicken breasts, bone and
  skin removed, cubed
8 ounces feta cheese, crumbled
Salt to taste

4 SERVINGS

Green Bean Chicken Skillet

INGREDIENTS

3 tablespoons margarine or butter, divided

2 cups rotisserie chicken breast cut into ¾-inch pieces

1 2.8-ounce can French fried onions, divided

1¼ cups cold water

¾ cup whole milk

1 4.7-ounce package pasta with cheese side dish mix

1 14.5-ounce can French-style green beans, drained

4 SERVINGS

1 Heat 1 tablespoon margarine in a large skillet over medium-high heat. Add chicken and 1½ cups French fried onions. Cook and stir 2 minutes; remove from skillet and set aside.

2 Add water, milk, 2 tablespoons margarine, pasta and contents of seasoning packet to the same skillet. Bring to a boil. Reduce heat to low. Gently boil, uncovered, 4 minutes, stirring occasionally.

3 Stir in chicken mixture and green beans; simmer, stirring frequently, until pasta is tender, about 2 to 4 minutes. Sprinkle evenly with remaining French fried onions. Serve hot. Refrigerate leftovers.

Not the traditional green bean casserole, but delicious. Serve with a side of sliced ripe tomatoes, cucumbers and crusty bread.

Lasagna Skillet

1 Spray a 12-inch nonstick skillet with cooking spray. Add sausage, onion, bell pepper, mushrooms and seasoning; cook and stir over medium-high heat until sausage is no longer pink; drain. Add chicken; stir and cook 1 minute.

2 Add noodles, water and pasta sauce. Bring mixture to a boil, stirring occasionally. Reduce heat; cover and simmer until pasta is tender, about 10 minutes.

3 Sprinkle with cheese. Serve hot. Refrigerate leftovers.

Serve with a green salad and warm garlic bread.

Variation: Use bow tie pasta instead of mafalda pasta.

INGREDIENTS

½ pound bulk Italian sausage
½ cup chopped yellow onion
1 green bell pepper, sliced
3 cups sliced fresh mushrooms
½ teaspoon Italian seasoning
2 cups diced rotisserie chicken, skin removed
3 cups mini-lasagna noodles (mafalda)
2½ cups water
1 26-ounce jar chunky tomato and basil pasta sauce
1 cup shredded mozzarella cheese

4 SERVINGS

Mac and Cheese with Chicken

INGREDIENTS

8 ounces whole wheat elbow
  macaroni
1 cup whole milk
2 tablespoons all-purpose flour
1 teaspoon dry mustard
Pinch of cayenne pepper, optional
1 cup shredded sharp Cheddar cheese
¼ cup shredded Parmesan cheese
1 cup diced rotisserie chicken,
  skin removed
Salt and black pepper to taste

4 SERVINGS

1 Cook macaroni according to package directions to al dente.

2 While pasta is cooking, whisk milk, flour, mustard and cayenne pepper in a large saucepan until well blended; cook over medium heat stirring constantly until thickened, about 6 to 8 minutes.

3 Add Cheddar and Parmesan cheeses; stir until melted. Stir in diced chicken. Add cooked drained pasta. Season with salt and pepper to taste. Serve. Refrigerate leftovers.

Serve with a side of buttered green beans.

Variation: Prepare a 7.5-ounce box of macaroni and cheese mix; add chicken.

Pasta with Chicken and Roasted Pepper Cream Sauce

1 Cook fettuccine according to package directions. Drain and keep warm.

2 Process peppers in food processor or blender to ¼-inch in size. Transfer to a large nonstick skillet.

3 Add sauce and chicken to skillet. Cook over medium-low heat, stirring occasionally, until heated through (do not boil).

4 Add cooked pasta to skillet; toss until coated. Serve hot, topped with cheese and chopped parsley as desired. Refrigerate leftovers.

Serve this quick-to-prepare entrée with a green salad and warm, crusty bread.

INGREDIENTS

1 9-ounce package refrigerated fettuccine
1 7.5-ounce jar roasted red peppers, drained
1 10-ounce container refrigerated light Alfredo sauce
2 cups boneless, skinless rotisserie chicken breast strips
Shredded Parmesan cheese
Chopped fresh parsley

4 SERVINGS

Pasta with Mushrooms and Chicken

INGREDIENTS

12 ounces dried orecchiette pasta
2 tablespoons olive oil
2 cups cubed rotisserie chicken breast, skin removed
1 cup finely chopped red onion
1 cup stemmed and thinly sliced shiitake mushrooms
1 large portobello mushroom cap, chopped
1 cup sugar snap peas or snow peas, strings removed
1 cup thinly sliced green onions
½ cup grated Parmesan cheese
¼ teaspoon salt
¼ teaspoon ground black pepper

4 SERVINGS

1 Cook pasta according to package directions; drain well, reserving ½ cup cooking water; keep warm.

2 Heat olive oil in a large skillet over medium-high heat. Add chicken; stir and cook 1 minute, then remove from skillet and place in a small bowl.

3 Add onion to skillet; cook and stir 1 minute. Add mushrooms; cook and stir until tender about 5 minutes. Add peas; cook until just tender, about 2 minutes. Return chicken to skillet; stir to combine.

4 Transfer skillet mixture, green onions, cheese, salt and pepper to a large bowl. Add pasta; toss well. Add some warm reserved pasta water, if needed, for moisture. Serve hot. Refrigerate leftovers.

Orecchiette pasta is named for its ear-like shape, and is perfect to hold the sauce. Small shell pasta may be substituted, if desired. Serve with warm, crusty rolls.

Quick Pad Thai

1 Heat 2 tablespoons corn oil in a large nonstick skillet. Add egg; scramble lightly for about 30 seconds. Add shrimp; stir and cook about 4 minutes or until pink. Add chicken; stir and cook 2 minutes.

2 Add remaining 2 tablespoons corn oil. Drain and add noodles; stir and cook 5 to 7 minutes or until noodles are tender but still firm.

3 Add green onions, sauce and bean sprouts; stir and cook 1 to 2 minutes or until all ingredients are hot. Sprinkle with peanuts and serve immediately. Refrigerate leftovers.

Serve this tasty dish with a side of fresh sliced melon.

INGREDIENTS

4 tablespoons corn oil, divided
1 egg, beaten
½ pound raw shrimp, peeled and deveined
1 cup finely cubed rotisserie chicken breast, skin removed
1 8-ounce package rice noodles, soaked according to package directions
4 green onions, sliced
1 3.25-ounce package Pad Thai sauce
2 cups bean sprouts
⅓ cup chopped peanuts

2 SERVINGS

Ravioli with Chicken in Mushroom Sauce

INGREDIENTS

1 tablespoon butter
4 cups sliced baby bella mushrooms
2 9-ounce containers refrigerated
　Alfredo sauce
1 ½ cups shredded rotisserie chicken,
　skin removed
1 11-ounce package refrigerated
　4 cheese ravioli
½ cup shredded Italian blend cheese
Torn fresh basil

4 SERVINGS

Preheat broiler.

1 Melt butter in a large skillet; cook until light golden brown. Add mushrooms; stir and cook about 5 minutes over medium heat or until cooked through. Stir in Alfredo sauce and chicken; simmer over low heat for 5 minutes. Remove from heat; keep warm.

2 Cook ravioli according to package directions; drain well. Spoon into an 11x7-inch baking dish. Pour warm sauce mixture over the top and sprinkle with cheese. Place in oven and broil until cheese is melted and starting to turn brown. Remove from oven. Sprinkle with basil. Serve. Refrigerate leftovers.

Serve with a crisp salad and warm bread.

Variation: Use shiitake or cremini mushrooms instead of baby bella.

Chicken Parmesan Skillet

1 Mix bread crumbs and Parmesan cheese in a food-grade plastic bag. Stir chicken into beaten egg. Add chicken to bread crumb mixture. Seal bag and shake until chicken is coated with bread crumbs.

2 Spray a 12-inch skillet with cooking spray. Add chicken; cook over medium-high heat, stirring occasionally, until browned.

3 Add pasta sauce; bring to a boil, then reduce heat to low. Stir in cheese and simmer until cheese is melted. Serve hot, over angel hair pasta. Refrigerate leftovers.

Serve this quick skillet meal with a crisp green salad and warm bread.

INGREDIENTS

¼ cup dried bread crumbs
¼ cup grated Parmesan cheese
2 cups large cubes of rotisserie chicken, skin removed
1 egg, beaten
1 26-ounce jar pasta sauce
1 cup shredded mozzarella cheese
Hot, cooked angel hair pasta

4 SERVINGS

Sesame Noodles with Chicken

INGREDIENTS

8 ounces linguine
1 cup matchstick-cut carrots
⅔ cup vegetable broth
½ cup reduced-fat peanut butter
2 tablespoons rice vinegar
2 tablespoons soy sauce
1 tablespoon bottled ground ginger
2 teaspoons hot chili sauce
2 cups chopped rotisserie chicken
  breast, skin removed
1 cup thinly sliced green onions
2 tablespoons sesame seeds, toasted

5 SERVINGS

1 Cook pasta according to package directions, omitting salt. Add carrots to pasta during the last 2 minutes of cooking. Drain well.

2 Mix broth, peanut butter, vinegar, soy sauce, ginger and chili sauce in a food processor; process until smooth.

3 Combine pasta mixture, chicken and onions in a large bowl. Drizzle broth mixture over pasta mixture; toss well. Sprinkle with sesame seeds. Serve hot. Refrigerate leftovers.

Serve this tasty dish along with a side of fresh sliced cucumbers and tomatoes.

Shells with Chicken and Ham

1 Bring water to a boil in a medium saucepan; add margarine. Reduce heat to medium. Slowly stir in shells. Boil, uncovered, 12 to 14 minutes, stirring frequently, or until most of the water is absorbed.

2 Stir in milk, chicken, ham, peas, mustard and contents of seasoning packet. Return to a boil. Boil 1 to 2 minutes or until pasta is tender. Let stand a few minutes for sauce to thicken.

3 Gently stir in tomatoes. Add salt and pepper to taste. Serve. Refrigerate leftovers.

Serve this creamy meal along with green salad and with soft, warm rolls.

INGREDIENTS

2 cups cold water
2 tablespoons margarine
1 6.2-ounce package shells and white
    Cheddar pasta mix
⅔ cup whole milk
1 cup diced rotisserie chicken breast
1 cup chopped fully cooked ham
1 cup frozen peas
2 teaspoons prepared mustard
1 cup cherry tomato halves
Salt and black pepper to taste

4 SERVINGS

Shrimp and Chicken Scampi

INGREDIENTS

1 pound linguine
¼ cup butter (no substitute)
2 tablespoons extra virgin olive oil
1 pound raw shrimp, peeled and
  deveined
1½ cups finely cubed rotisserie chicken
  breast, skin removed
4 cloves garlic, minced
½ teaspoon grated lemon zest
3 tablespoons fresh lemon juice
3 tablespoons white wine
½ cup snipped flat leaf parsley or
  fresh basil
Salt and pepper to taste
Parmesan cheese, optional

6 SERVINGS

1 Cook linguine according to package directions; drain and keep warm.

2 Heat butter and olive oil in a large nonstick skillet over medium heat. Add shrimp; cook and stir until fully pink. Add chicken and garlic; cook and stir 2 minutes.

3 Stir in lemon zest, lemon juice and wine; cook and stir 2 minutes. Stir in parsley or basil, salt and pepper to taste.

4 Add cooked pasta to skillet; toss until coated. Serve topped with Parmesan cheese as desired. Serve immediately. Refrigerate leftovers.

Crusty bread and a green salad are the perfect partners for this delicious dish.

Tex-Mex Chicken Spaghetti

1 Cook pasta according to package directions; drain and keep warm.

2 Heat olive oil in a large skillet over medium heat. Add onion; cook and stir 5 minutes. Add chicken and salsa; bring to a simmer. Stir in Alfredo sauce.

3 Add cooked pasta to mixture; toss until mixture is coated and hot. Serve immediately, topped with cheese and avocados. Refrigerate leftovers.

A quick and delicious main dish. Serve with warm, crusty bread.

INGREDIENTS

- 1 16-ounce package spaghetti
- 2 tablespoons olive oil
- 1 medium onion, chopped
- 2 cups chopped rotisserie chicken, skin removed
- 1 16-ounce jar chunky salsa
- 1 15-ounce jar four cheese Alfredo sauce
- ½ cup grated Parmesan cheese, or to taste
- 2 avocados, peeled, pitted and chopped

6 SERVINGS

Thai Chicken Fettuccine

INGREDIENTS

6 ounces fettuccine
1 cup mild picante sauce
¼ cup orange juice
2 tablespoons honey
1 tablespoon chunky peanut butter
1 tablespoon soy sauce
½ teaspoon ground ginger
1½ cups cubed rotisserie chicken
  breast, skin removed

4 SERVINGS

1 Cook fettuccine according to package directions. Drain and keep warm.

2 Mix picante sauce, orange juice, honey, peanut butter, soy sauce and ginger in a medium-sized saucepan. Cook over low heat, stirring occasionally, until well blended, about 5 minutes.

3 Stir in chicken; cook and stir until heated through, about 5 minutes. Place mixture in a large bowl. Add cooked fettuccine; toss. Serve warm. Refrigerate leftovers.

Garnish this zesty pasta dish with peanut halves, pepper strips and cilantro when serving.

Stove-Top Main Dishes with Rice

Apricot Chicken Curry

INGREDIENTS

1 ½ tablespoons margarine
½ cup chopped onion
3 cloves garlic, minced
1 tablespoon curry powder
2 cups bite-sized pieces rotisserie
   chicken breast, skin removed
¼ cup apricot preserves
1 apple, cored and cut into
   bite-sized pieces
¼ cup dark raisins
⅓ cup water
¼ teaspoon salt
1 ½ cups plain low-fat yogurt, mixed in
   a cup with 2 tablespoons cornstarch
Hot, cooked rice

4 SERVINGS

1 Heat margarine in a large nonstick skillet over medium-high heat. Add onion, garlic and curry powder; stir and cook 1 minute. Add chicken; cook and stir about 2 minutes.

2 Stir in preserves, apple, raisins, water and salt. Add yogurt mixture; stir until thickened and bubbly. Cook and stir 3 minutes more. Serve hot over rice. Refrigerate leftovers.

Serve with a spinach or green garden salad.

Broccoli and Chicken Skillet

1 Heat corn oil in a large skillet over medium-high heat. Add onions and garlic; cook and stir 2 minutes.

2 Add broccoli, carrots, water chestnuts and water. Cook about 9 minutes, stirring occasionally, or until vegetables are crisp-tender and water is gone.

3 Add teriyaki glaze and chicken; stir gently and cook until chicken is thoroughly heated, about 3 minutes. Serve rice. Refrigerate leftovers.

I keep cooked rice in my freezer; it's easy to microwave it and serve hot. Cooked rice can also be found in the freezer section of your supermarket.

INGREDIENTS

2 tablespoons corn oil
½ cup finely chopped yellow onion
4 cloves garlic, chopped
4 cups fresh broccoli florets
2 small carrots cut lengthwise then cut in half
1 8-ounce can sliced water chestnuts, drained
¼ cup water
½ cup bottled teriyaki glaze sauce
2 cups thin rotisserie breast strips, skin removed
Hot, cooked rice

4 SERVINGS

Broccoli and Chicken Stir-Fry

INGREDIENTS

1½ tablespoons corn oil
1 small yellow onion, cut into thin wedges
3 cloves garlic, finely chopped
1 small red bell pepper cut into thin strips
2 cups cubed rotisserie chicken breast, skin removed
1 teaspoon Chinese five spice powder
2 cups fresh broccoli florets
1 8-ounce can sliced water chestnuts, drained
1 6-ounce package frozen snow peas, thawed
1 14-ounce container chicken broth
2 tablespoons cornstarch
2 tablespoons cold water
4 cups hot, cooked white rice

4 SERVINGS

1 Heat oil in a large nonstick skillet. Add onion, garlic and bell pepper; cook and stir 3 minutes. Add chicken and Chinese five spice seasoning; cook and stir 1 minute.

2 Add broccoli, water chestnuts and snow peas; cook, stirring occasionally, until broccoli is crisp-tender, about 8 minutes.

3 Stir in broth. Mix cornstarch and water in a small bowl until smooth. Gradually stir mixture into chicken mixture. Cook and stir until thickened, about 2 minutes. Serve hot over rice. Refrigerate leftovers.

Rice will take 20 minutes to cook from scratch, so start rice first, then the stir-fry.

Tip: Frozen cooked rice can be found in the freezer section of the supermarket.

Cheddar and Chicken Skillet

1 In a large nonstick skillet over medium heat, sauté rice-vermicelli mix according to package directions.

2 Slowly stir in 2 cups cold water. Stir in basil and contents of seasoning packet. Bring mixture to a boil. Cover; reduce heat to low. Simmer 10 minutes; stir. Top evenly with chicken; cover and cook 5 minutes.

3 Top evenly with chopped tomatoes and green onions; cover and cook until heated through, about 5 minutes. Remove from heat; sprinkle evenly with cheese. Serve hot. Refrigerate leftovers.

A packaged rice mix is used to prepare this quick main meal. Serve with a crisp green salad.

INGREDIENTS

1 6.9-ounce package chicken-flavored rice-vermicelli mix, such as Rice-a-Roni®
2 cups cold water
1 teaspoon dried basil leaves
2 cups thin strips of rotisserie chicken breast, skin removed
1 cup chopped fresh tomatoes
¼ cup sliced green onions
½ cup (2 ounces) shredded Cheddar cheese

4 SERVINGS

Chicken and Pea Pods

INGREDIENTS

2 tablespoons corn oil
1 medium yellow onion, chopped
5 cloves fresh garlic, chopped
3 cups long, thin strips of rotisserie
  chicken breast, skin removed
Salt and black pepper to taste
3 stalks celery, diagonally sliced
½ pound fresh snow pea pods, ends
  snipped
1 8-ounce package fresh mushrooms,
  sliced and sautéed in butter in a
  small skillet, then drained
3 cups low-sodium chicken broth
3 tablespoons cornstarch, mixed in a
  small bowl with ¼ cup cold water
1 8-ounce can sliced water chestnuts
Hot, cooked long grain white rice

4 SERVINGS

1 Heat corn oil in a large nonstick skillet over medium-high heat. Add onion and garlic; cook and stir until soft. Add chicken, salt and pepper; stir and cook 2 minutes. Add celery and pea pods; stir and cook 2 minutes. Add mushrooms and broth. Stir in cornstarch mixture until well blended. Stir in water chestnuts.

2 Cook mixture over medium heat, stirring often, until pea pods are crisp-tender, about 9 minutes. Add water if too thick. A thin sauce is desired. Serve immediately over rice. Refrigerate leftovers.

This is a favorite dish at our house . . . usually cooked by my husband!

Tip: The rice will take 20 minutes to cook, so put rice on first, and then start the chicken dish. Cooked white rice is available in the freezer section of the supermarket.

Chicken Chow Mein

1 Heat corn oil in a large skillet over medium-high heat. Add onion, garlic and celery; stir and cook until crisp-tender, about 3 minutes. Add chicken; stir and cook 2 minutes. Remove from skillet; set aside.

2 Add chicken broth; bring to a boil. Stir in cornstarch mixture until smooth and is thickened.

3 Return chicken mixture and remaining ingredients to skillet. Cover and simmer 10 minutes. Serve hot, over rice. Refrigerate leftovers.

Serve this skillet chow mein over hot, cooked white rice and chow mein noodles.

INGREDIENTS

1 tablespoon corn oil
1 medium yellow onion, thinly sliced
3 cloves fresh garlic, chopped
2 cups diagonally sliced celery
2 cups thinly sliced rotisserie chicken breast strips, lightly seasoned with salt, black pepper and a pinch of garlic powder
1 10-ounce can condensed chicken broth
2 tablespoons cornstarch mixed in a cup with ½ cup cold water
1 7-ounce can sliced water chestnuts, drained
1 4-ounce can sliced mushrooms, drained
1 cup bean sprouts, fresh or canned
3 tablespoons soy sauce
Hot, cooked rice

4 SERVINGS

Chicken Fried Rice

INGREDIENTS

2 tablespoons corn oil, divided
3 eggs, beaten
2 cloves garlic, minced
8 green onions, sliced diagonally into
   1 inch pieces
1 cup sliced fresh mushrooms
2½ cups diced rotisserie chicken,
   skin removed
3 cups cold cooked rice
2 tablespoons soy sauce mixed with
   ⅛ teaspoon black pepper
½ cup frozen peas, thawed and
   drained
½ cup fresh bean sprouts, rinsed
   and drained

4 SERVINGS

1 Heat 1 tablespoon corn oil in a large nonstick skillet over medium-high heat until very hot. Add eggs. Lift and tilt skillet to form a thin sheet of egg. Cook without stirring until just set. Slide cooked egg onto a cutting board and shred with a knife; set aside.

2 Heat 1 tablespoon corn oil in same skillet over medium-high heat. Add garlic; stir and cook for a few seconds. Add green onions and mushrooms; stir and cook 2 minutes. Remove vegetables from skillet; set aside.

3 Add chicken to same skillet (add more oil if necessary); stir and cook 2 minutes.

4 Add rice; stir and cook 2 minute. Stir in soy sauce, peas, bean sprouts, cooked vegetables and shredded egg. Stir and cook until all ingredients are heated through. Serve hot. Refrigerate leftovers.

Almost take-out! Serve with a side of purchased egg rolls.

Chicken Jambalaya with Shrimp

1 Heat corn oil in a 4-quart heavy saucepan over medium heat. Add onion, celery and carrots. Cover and cook 5 minutes, stirring occasionally. Add sausage; cook 2 minutes.

2 Stir in rice, tomatoes, chicken broth, shrimp, chicken, salt and black pepper. Cover and cook 8 minutes. Remove from heat; fluff with a fork. Serve immediately. Refrigerate leftovers.

A hearty combination of good things from Cajun country. Serve with a mixed greens salad and warm French bread.

INGREDIENTS

2 tablespoons corn oil
1 cup diced yellow onion
½ cup thinly sliced celery
½ cup diced carrots
1 12-ounce package andouille or other fully cooked smoked sausage, cut into 1-inch pieces
2 cups cooked white rice
1 14-ounce can diced tomatoes with green chiles
1 cup low-sodium chicken broth
1 pound medium-sized raw shrimp, peeled and deveined
2 cups cubed rotisserie chicken breast, skin removed
Salt and black pepper to taste

4 SERVINGS

Chinese Chicken Fried Rice

INGREDIENTS

1 tablespoon sesame oil or corn oil
1 cup chopped yellow onion
3 cups cubed rotisserie chicken,
   skin removed
2 tablespoons soy sauce
2 large carrots, diced
2 stalks celery, chopped
1 large red bell pepper, diced
Half of a large green bell pepper, diced
¾ cup fresh snow pea pods, halved
   (ends snipped and discarded)
6 cups cold, cooked long grain
   white rice
2 large eggs, scrambled in a small
   skillet, set aside
¼ cup soy sauce, or to taste
1 cup fresh bean sprouts, cleaned

6 SERVINGS

1 Heat oil in a large nonstick skillet over medium heat. Add onion; cook and stir until soft. Add chicken and 2 tablespoons soy sauce; cook and stir 5 minutes.

2 Add carrots, celery, bell peppers and pea pods; cook and stir 5 minutes.

3 Stir in rice until well mixed. Stir in scrambled eggs and ¼ cup soy sauce or to taste. Stir in bean sprouts; cook and stir until heated through. Serve. Refrigerate leftovers.

Serve this stir-fry with a side of sliced melon.

Tip: Cooked rice can be found in the freezer section of your supermarket.

Chop Suey

1 Cook rice according to package directions.

2 Heat oil in a large nonstick skillet. Add onion; cook and stir for 2 minutes. Add chicken; cook and stir 2 minutes.

3 Add vegetables and water. Bring mixture to a boil, then reduce heat, cover and simmer, stirring occasionally, until vegetables are crisp-tender, about 7 minutes.

4 Stir in sir-fry sauce, honey, salt, pepper and ginger. Heat thoroughly.

5 Serve over hot, cooked rice and chow mein noodles; top with cashews.

This chicken chop suey is ready for the table in minutes.

INGREDIENTS

1 cup long grain rice, uncooked
1 tablespoon corn oil
½ cup chopped yellow onion
2½ cups diced rotisserie chicken, skin removed
1 16-ounce bag fresh stir-fry vegetables
½ cup water
½ cup basic stir-fry sauce
1 tablespoon honey
¼ teaspoon salt, or to taste
¼ teaspoon ground black pepper
⅛ teaspoon ground ginger
2 cups chow mein noodles
¼ cup cashew pieces or slivered almonds

4 SERVINGS

Creamy Chicken and Broccoli Skillet

INGREDIENTS

2½ cups cubed rotisserie chicken,
   skin removed
3 cups broccoli florets
8 ounces cubed processed American
   cheese
½ cup salad dressing, or mayonnaise
Hot, cooked rice

4 SERVINGS

1 Mix chicken, broccoli and cheese in a medium-sized nonstick skillet. Cover and cook over medium heat until broccoli is crisp-tender and cheese is melted. Stir in salad dressing; heat thoroughly, but do not boil.

2 Serve immediately over hot, cooked rice. Refrigerate leftovers.

This is a quick way to get supper on the table . . . very filling. Serve with a lettuce salad dressed with Italian dressing or with a side of sliced ripe tomatoes or both!

Garlic Chicken Ham Rice Skillet

1 Heat 1 tablespoon oil in a large skillet. Stir in eggs; cook and break into small pieces. Remove and set aside.

2 Heat remaining corn oil in same skillet. Cook and stir celery over medium heat until crisp-tender. Add garlic; cook and stir 2 minutes. Add rice, stirring constantly, and cook for 3 minutes.

3 Add chicken, ham, soy sauce, black pepper, ginger, eggs and green onions; stir until heated through. Serve hot. Refrigerate leftovers.

Cooked white rice is available in the frozen section of your super-market. Serve this flavorful dish with a lettuce and tomato salad.

INGREDIENTS

¼ cup corn oil, divided
2 eggs, scrambled in a small bowl
1 cup sliced celery
3 cloves garlic, finely chopped
4 cups cold cooked white rice
2 cups chopped rotisserie chicken
1 cup diced fully cooked ham
½ cup soy sauce
½ teaspoon ground black pepper
¼ teaspoon ground ginger, optional
3 green onions, sliced

4 SERVINGS

Greek Chicken Skillet

INGREDIENTS

1 6.9-ounce package chicken-flavored
   rice-vermicelli mix, such as
   Rice-A-Roni®
2 tablespoons margarine
2½ cups water
2 cups chopped rotisserie chicken,
   skin removed
1 medium green bell pepper, chopped
½ cup chopped onion
2 cloves garlic, minced
1 teaspoon dried oregano leaves
2 large plum tomatoes, chopped
⅓ cup ripe or Kalamata olive slices
Crumbled Feta cheese or shredded
   Italian cheese blend

4 SERVINGS

1 Stir rice-vermicelli mix (do not add seasoning packet) and margarine in a large skillet over medium heat until golden brown.

2 Slowly stir in water and seasoning packet; bring to a boil. Cover, then reduce heat and simmer 10 minutes.

3 Stir in chicken, bell pepper, onions, garlic and oregano. Cover and simmer 10 minutes. Stir in tomatoes and olives; cook until heated through.

4 Sprinkle with cheese as desired. Serve hot. Refrigerate leftovers.

Serve this tasty skillet with a crisp green salad.

Japanese Teriyaki Chicken and Rice

1 Place carrots, orange juice and ginger in a small nonstick saucepan. Cover and cook over medium heat 5 minutes.

2 Stir in teriyaki sauce, chicken and mushrooms. Bring mixture to a boil. Cook, stirring frequently, until mushrooms are tender, about 3 minutes. Stir in green onions, salt and pepper.

3 Mound 1 cup hot, cooked rice each in 4 individual bowls. Top equally with chicken mixture. Serve hot. Serve with steamed pea pods, if desired. Refrigerate leftovers.

White rice will take 20 minutes to cook, so start the rice first, then the chicken dish.

Variation: Use other mushrooms instead of button.

Tip: Cooked white rice can be found in the freezer section of the supermarket.

INGREDIENTS

1 cup carrots thinly sliced and
   quartered
½ cup fresh orange juice
Pinch ground ginger
1 12-ounce bottle teriyaki sauce
3 cups diced rotisserie chicken breast,
   skin removed
1 ½ cups sliced button mushrooms
¼ cup thinly sliced green onion
Salt and black pepper to taste
4 cups hot, cooked white rice
Steamed pea pods, optional

4 SERVINGS

Lentils and Chicken Skillet

INGREDIENTS

2 teaspoons corn oil
1 small yellow onion, minced
1½ teaspoons curry powder
1 15-ounce can lentils, rinsed
1 14-ounce can diced fire-roasted
  tomatoes
4 cups coarsely chopped rotisserie
  chicken, skin removed
¼ teaspoon salt or to taste
¼ cup low-fat plain yogurt
Hot, cooked rice

4 SERVINGS

1 Heat corn oil in a large heavy saucepan over medium-high heat. Add onions; cook and stir until softened but not browned, about 3 minutes.

2 Stir in curry powder until well blended. Stir in lentils, tomatoes, chicken and salt. Cook, stirring mixture often, until heated through.

3 Remove from heat; stir in yogurt. Serve immediately over rice. Refrigerate leftovers.

Serve along with a green salad.

Moose's Chicken Stir-Fry

1 Heat corn oil in a heavy nonstick skillet over medium-high heat. Add chicken; cook and stir 1 minute.

2 Add vegetables and salt; cook and stir 5 minutes. Stir in broth; cook and stir 3 minutes. Serve immediately over hot, cooked white rice or cooked thin spaghetti. Refrigerate leftovers.

Chicken thighs are used in this quick meal. Serve with a salad of bagged mixed greens.

INGREDIENTS

1 tablespoon corn oil
2 cubed rotisserie chicken thighs, skin removed, seasoned with just a pinch of garlic powder and a pinch of ground black pepper
1½ cups small cauliflower florets
1½ cups small broccoli florets
1 cup thinly sliced fresh carrots
1 cup sliced green onions, tops included
¼ teaspoon salt, or to taste
½ cup chicken broth, heated
Hot, cooked rice or thin spaghetti

4 SERVINGS

Quick Chicken Fried Rice

INGREDIENTS

1 6.2-ounce package fried rice mix
2 cups cubed rotisserie chicken, skin removed
1 ½ cups broccoli florets, cooked crisp-tender
1 8-ounce can sliced water chestnuts, drained
1 cup shredded mozzarella cheese

6 SERVINGS

1 Cook rice mix according to package directions.

2 Stir in chicken, broccoli and water chestnuts; heat thoroughly. Top with cheese. Serve hot. Refrigerate leftovers.

Packaged fried rice mix makes short work of this chicken supper. Serve with fresh slices of cantaloupe or other fresh melon.

Rice and Vegetable Chicken Skillet

1 Prepare rice according to package directions for range top.

2 While rice is cooking, heat olive oil in a large nonstick skillet. Add onion, garlic and green pepper. Stir and cook over medium heat for 5 minutes.

3 Add broccoli, cauliflower, zucchini, yellow squash, salt and pepper. Cook and stir over medium heat until vegetables are crisp-tender, about 10 to 15 minutes.

4 Add cubed chicken; gently stir and cook until heated through.

5 Add cooked rice to skillet; toss gently to combine. Serve hot. Refrigerate leftovers.

Serve with a plain lettuce salad, dressed with Italian salad dressing.

INGREDIENTS

1 5.9-once package chicken and garlic rice-and-vermicelli mix, such as Rice-a-Roni®
1½ tablespoons olive oil
1 cup sliced yellow onion
2 cloves fresh garlic, chopped
Half of a large green bell pepper, cut into thin strips
1 cup broccoli florets, thick pieces cut in half
1 cup thinly sliced cauliflower
1 small zucchini, sliced and quartered
1 small yellow squash, sliced and quartered
½ teaspoon salt, or to taste
¼ teaspoon ground black pepper
1 cubed rotisserie chicken breast half, skin removed

5 SERVINGS

Speedy Chicken Mole

INGREDIENTS

2 teaspoons olive oil
1 medium onion, chopped
2 cloves garlic, crushed with a press
2 teaspoons chili powder
2 teaspoons unsweetened
  cocoa powder
¼ teaspoon ground cinnamon
1¼ cups chicken broth
1 tablespoon creamy peanut butter
1 tablespoon tomato paste
¼ cup raisins
1 rotisserie chicken cut into 8 pieces
¼ cup chopped cilantro
Hot, cooked white rice

4 SERVINGS

1 Heat olive oil in a 12-inch nonstick skillet over medium heat. Add onion; cook and stir 5 minutes. Add garlic, chili powder, cocoa powder and cinnamon; cook and stir 1 minute.

2 Stir in chicken broth, peanut butter, tomato paste and raisins. Bring mixture to a boil.

3 Add chicken pieces. Reduce heat to medium-low. Cover and simmer 5 to 10 minutes, turning chicken over halfway through cooking to coat all sides with sauce. Sprinkle with cilantro. Serve hot over rice. Refrigerate leftovers.

Serve with a lettuce and avocado salad.

Spicy Chicken and Vegetable Stir-Fry

1 Heat corn oil in a large skillet. Cut larger broccoli pieces in half, then add to skillet along with remaining stir-fry vegetables. Stir and cook over medium high heat about 10 minutes or until vegetables are crisp-tender.

2 Stir in water chestnuts and sauces. Simmer mixture 2 minutes. Add chicken, and cook until mixture is very hot. Serve warm. Refrigerate leftovers.

Frozen vegetables and purchased sauces make this stir-fry quick and easy.

Variation: Serve over noodles instead of rice.

INGREDIENTS

2 tablespoons corn oil
1 16-ounce package frozen stir-fry vegetables (the kind with broccoli and snow peas), thawed
1 8-ounce can sliced water chestnuts, drained
½ cup teriyaki sauce
3 tablespoons Szechuan spicy stir-fry sauce
2 cups diced rotisserie chicken, skin removed
Hot, cooked rice

4 SERVINGS

Spicy Shrimp Chicken Stir-Fry

INGREDIENTS

2 teaspoons hot chili sesame oil
1 pound raw shrimp, peeled and
  deveined
2 cups diced rotisserie chicken breast,
  skin removed
4 cups cut-up stir-fry vegetables,
  chunked, such as broccoli, carrots,
  red or yellow bell peppers, onions
  and snow peas
2 tablespoons wasabi teriyaki sauce,
  or to taste
Hot, cooked white rice

4 SERVINGS

1 Heat oil over high heat in a wok or heavy skillet. Add shrimp; cook and stir until completely pink. Add chicken; stir and cook 1 minute. Remove shrimp and chicken from wok; set aside.

2 Add vegetables to wok; stir and cook until crisp-tender.

3 Return shrimp and chicken to wok. Add teriyaki sauce; cook until all ingredients are heated through, about 2 minutes. Serve over rice. Refrigerate leftovers.

No need for take-out tonight!

Szechuan Peach Chicken Stir-Fry

1 Heat corn oil in a large nonstick skillet, or a wok, over medium-high heat. Add onions; stir and cook 3 minutes. Add green pepper, peach and seasoning; stir and cook 5 minutes. Add chicken; stir and cook 1 minute.

2 Mix cornstarch, chicken broth and soy sauce in a small bowl until cornstarch is dissolved. Gradually add mixture to chicken mixture, stirring constantly, until sauce is thickened and clear, about 2 minutes. Serve over rice. Refrigerate leftovers

Serve this quick-to-prepare sweet and tangy stir-fry for a delicious supper.

INGREDIENTS

1 tablespoon corn oil
Half of a medium red onion, thinly sliced
1 green bell pepper, cut into thin strips
1 large fresh peach, peeled, pitted and sliced
1 teaspoon Szechuan seasoning
4 rotisserie chicken breast halves, cut into thin strips
2 teaspoons cornstarch
½ cup chicken broth
2 tablespoons soy sauce
4 cups hot, cooked white rice

4 SERVINGS

Zucchini Sausage Chicken Skillet

INGREDIENTS

2 tablespoons extra virgin olive oil
1 cup thinly sliced yellow onion
1 green bell pepper cut into thin strips
1 cup sliced zucchini
1 cup sliced fresh button mushrooms
¾ pound Italian link sausages, cut into
   ½ inch pieces
2½ cups cubed rotisserie chicken
   breast, skin removed
2 14.5-ounce cans diced tomatoes,
   undrained
1 clove garlic, minced
½ teaspoon dried oregano leaves
½ teaspoon dried basil leaves
Hot, cooked white rice

4 SERVINGS

1 Heat olive oil in a large nonstick skillet over medium heat. Add onion and bell pepper; cook and stir 2 minutes. Add zucchini and mushrooms; cook and stir until tender. Remove vegetables from skillet; set aside.

2 Add sausage to skillet. Cook until meat is no longer pink; drain fat from skillet. Add chicken; cook and stir 2 minutes.

3 Stir in tomatoes, garlic, oregano and basil. Return vegetables to skillet. Bring mixture to a boil. Reduce heat. Cover and simmer until heated through, about 10 minutes. Serve hot over rice. Refrigerate leftovers.

Serve with a crisp green salad.

Stove-Top Main Dishes – Other

Barbecued Chicken Burritos

INGREDIENTS

4 cups shredded rotisserie chicken,
  skin removed
½ cup prepared hot barbecue sauce
1 cup canned black beans, rinsed
  and drained
½ cup frozen corn, thawed, or drained
  canned corn
¼ cup reduced-fat sour cream
4 leaves romaine lettuce
4 (10-inch) whole wheat tortillas,
  warmed according to package
  directions
2 limes, cut into wedges

4 SERVINGS

1 Cook and stir chicken, barbecue sauce, beans, corn and sour cream in a large nonstick skillet over medium-high heat until mixture is hot, about 5 minutes.

2 Place a lettuce leaf in center of each tortilla, then top each with one-quarter of the chicken mixture. Roll as a burrito. Slice in half diagonally and serve warm with lime wedges. Refrigerate leftovers.

Whole wheat tortillas are used for these tangy burritos. Serve with a spinach avocado salad or fresh cantaloupe.

Chicken and Vegetable Skillet

1 Heat oil in a 12-inch skillet over medium-high heat. Add chicken; cook and stir 2 minutes. Remove from skillet; set aside.

2 Stir sauce, vegetables and cheese together in same skillet. Bring mixture to a boil. Reduce heat to low. Cover and cook 15 minutes or until vegetables are crisp-tender.

3 Return chicken to skillet; cook until heated through. Season with salt and pepper to taste. Serve hot over spaghetti. Refrigerate leftovers.

Serve with a green salad dressed with Italian salad dressing.

Variation: Use linguine instead of spaghetti.

INGREDIENTS

1 tablespoon corn oil
2 boneless, skinless, garlic-flavored
    rotisserie chicken breast halves,
    cut into strips
1 24-ounce jar mushroom pasta sauce,
1 16-ounce bag frozen vegetable
    combination (broccoli, cauliflower
    and carrots)
¼ cup grated Parmesan cheese
Salt and black pepper to taste
16 ounces spaghetti, cooked
    according to package directions

6 SERVINGS

Chicken Egg Foo Young

INGREDIENTS

Sauce
1 tablespoon cornstarch
2 tablespoons cold water
1 cup chicken stock
¼ cup soy sauce
1 teaspoon hot sauce
Pinch of ground ginger
8 eggs, beaten in a large bowl
1 cup finely chopped rotisserie
   chicken breast, skin removed
¼ pound fully cooked ham, finely
   chopped
1 cup fresh bean sprouts
½ cup finely shredded carrots
1 cup mushrooms, thinly sliced
1 cup baby bok choy, finely shredded
1 8-ounce can water chestnuts,
   drained and finely chopped
½ cup very thinly sliced red
   bell pepper
1 bunch green onions (white and
   green parts) very thinly sliced at
   an angle
½ teaspoon grated ginger root
2 cloves fresh garlic, grated
½ teaspoon salt
¼ teaspoon ground black pepper

4 SERVINGS

Preheat and oil griddle.

1 Mix cornstarch and water in a cup until smooth; pour into a small saucepan. Stir in chicken stock, soy sauce, hot sauce and ginger. Bring to a boil. Reduce heat to medium; cook and stir until mixture is thickened, about 3 minutes. Remove from heat.

2 Stir all remaining ingredients in a large bowl. Drop about ½ cup mixture onto prepared griddle. Cook (like a pancake) until golden, about 2 to 3 minutes on each side. Serve topped with sauce. Refrigerate leftovers.

Serve with a side of hot, cooked white rice or chicken fried rice.

Chipotle Chile Burritos

1 Tear chicken meat into bite-sized pieces. Place in a large sauce-pan with salsa, chiles and adobo sauce. Cook over medium-low heat 2 to 3 minutes or until warm.

2 Warm tortillas. Place equal amounts of chicken mixture and cheese in each tortilla.

3 Add rice, beans, onions, sour cream and guacamole, as desired. Roll up and serve. Refrigerate leftovers.

Serve with a side of fresh melon wedges or grapes.

INGREDIENTS

1 rotisserie chicken, skin and bones discarded
2 7-ounce cans salsa verde
2 tablespoons canned minced chipotle chiles in adobo sauce
1 tablespoon adobo sauce from can
1 8-ounce package Mexican style shredded cheese
6 10-inch flour tortillas
Warm Spanish rice
Warm black beans
Sliced green onions
Sour cream
Guacamole

6 SERVINGS

Easy Chicken Enchilada

INGREDIENTS

1 tablespoon corn oil
1 cup chopped white onion
1 cup chopped bell pepper
1 10-ounce can enchilada sauce
2 cups chopped rotisserie chicken,
  skin removed
1 cup reduced-fat Mexican blend
  cheese, divided
½ teaspoon cumin
8 (6-inch) corn tortillas
Sour cream
Chopped fresh cilantro, optional

4 SERVINGS

Preheat broiler.

1 Heat corn oil in a large skillet over medium-high heat. Add onion and bell pepper; cook and stir until crisp-tender, about 2 minutes. Stir in enchilada sauce. Bring mixture to a boil, then reduce heat. Cover and simmer 5 minutes.

2 Mix chicken, ¾ cup cheese and cumin in a bowl.

3 Wrap tortillas in paper towels; microwave on high for 30 seconds or until warm.

4 Spoon ¼ cup chicken mixture across the center of each tortilla; roll up. Place tortillas, seam sides down, in an 11x7-inch baking dish coated with cooking spray.

5 Pour sauce mixture evenly over enchiladas. Sprinkle with remaining ¼ cup cheese. Broil 1 minute or until cheese melts. Serve. Top each serving with sour cream and cilantro as desired. Refrigerate leftovers.

Serve with a side of warm refried beans.

Easy Chicken Primavera

1 Heat butter in a large nonstick skillet over medium-high heat. Add chicken and garlic; cook and stir 5 minutes.

2 Stir in whipping cream and frozen vegetables and pasta. Reduce heat. Cover and simmer abut 8 minutes or until vegetables are crisp-tender. Serve immediately. Refrigerate leftovers.

Serve with green salad and warm French bread or hard rolls.

Refried Beans and Chicken Burritos

INGREDIENTS

1 tablespoon corn oil
2 rotisserie chicken breasts, cubed
⅛ teaspoon garlic powder
⅛ teaspoon ground black pepper
1 cup enchilada sauce
1 16 ounce can refried beans
8 (10-inch) flour tortillas, warmed
2 cups shredded lettuce
1 cup shredded Cheddar cheese
½ cup sliced green onions
Sour cream
Mild salsa

8 BURRITOS

1 Heat corn oil in medium-sized nonstick skillet over medium heat. Add chicken; sprinkle with garlic powder and black pepper. Stir and cook 2 minutes.

2 Stir in enchilada sauce; cook, stirring occasionally, 6 minutes. Stir in beans; cook and stir until heated through, about 2 minutes.

3 Spread about ½ cup hot mixture across the center of each warmed tortilla. Top with lettuce, cheese and green onions and then roll up. Garnish with sour cream and salsa as desired. Serve. Refrigerate leftovers.

Quick and tasty; serve with a side of flavored rice.

Shrimp and Chicken Stir-Fry

1 Heat corn oil in a large nonstick skillet over high heat.

2 Add the next six ingredients to skillet. Stir and cook about 3 minutes or until shrimp turn pink.

3 Add bean sprouts and chicken broth; cover and steam 2 minutes.

4 Mix cornstarch and soy sauce in a cup until dissolved; gradually add mixture to skillet, stirring constantly, until thickened, about 1 minute. Serve hot. Refrigerate leftovers.

Serve this delicious stir-fry, filled with crunchy vegetables, over hot, cooked rice.

INGREDIENTS

2½ tablespoons corn oil
1 pound medium shrimp, shelled and deveined
1 cup finely cubed rotisserie chicken breast, skin removed
¾ cup fresh broccoli florets
2 fresh carrots, thinly sliced
2 cloves garlic, minced
1 (½-inch) piece ginger, minced
1 cup fresh bean sprouts
¾ cup chicken broth
1 tablespoon cornstarch
2 tablespoons soy sauce

6 SERVINGS

Quinoa and Chicken

INGREDIENTS

1 cup quinoa, rinsed under cold
  water and drained
2 cups cold water
1 tablespoon extra virgin olive oil
½ cup finely chopped red onion
½ pound fresh asparagus cut into
  1-inch pieces
2 cloves garlic, finely chopped
1 cup fresh peas, or frozen petite
  peas, thawed
1 cup shredded rotisserie chicken,
  skin removed
1 cup thinly sliced baby spinach leaves
Salt and ground black pepper to taste

4 SERVINGS

1 Stir quinoa and 2 cups water in a medium saucepan. Bring to a boil, then reduce heat to simmer. Cover and cook until tender and all water is absorbed, about 15 minutes.

2 Heat olive oil in a large skillet over medium heat. Add onion and asparagus; cook and stir 5 minutes. Add garlic and peas; cook and stir 5 minutes.

3 Stir in chicken and cooked quinoa. Add spinach; cook and stir until just wilted. Season with salt and pepper to taste. Serve immediately. Refrigerate leftovers.

Quinoa is a grain-like seed, rising in popularity. Fresh asparagus, peas and baby spinach are featured in this dish.

Sauces, Glazes & Salsas

Apricot Balsamic Glaze

INGREDIENTS

2 tablespoons unsalted butter
½ cup apricot preserves
3 tablespoons balsamic vinegar
½ teaspoon crushed red pepper flakes
¼ cup chopped fresh rosemary
Pinch of kosher salt

MAKES 1 CUP

1 Melt butter in a small saucepan over medium heat. Stir in preserves, vinegar, red pepper flakes, rosemary and salt. Bring to a boil; reduce heat to medium-low and simmer, stirring occasionally, until slightly thickened, about 4 minutes. Remove from heat; cool to room temperature. Serve. Refrigerate leftovers.

Serve over warm, whole chicken pieces. If making ahead of time, store covered in the refrigerator. Warm over low heat when using.

Mango Salsa with Black Beans

1 Mix all ingredients in a medium-sized serving bowl until just combined. Test for seasoning and adjust, if needed. Serve. Refrigerate leftovers.

*Do not touch your eyes when working with jalapeños!

Serve with cold chicken sandwiches.

 Tip: Do not over-mix the salsa or it will become mushy.

INGREDIENTS

½ cup black beans, rinsed and drained
1 ripe medium mango, peeled, pitted and diced into ¼-inch pieces
1 medium red bell pepper, diced
Half of a red onion, diced
8 tablespoons pineapple juice
⅓ cup finely chopped fresh cilantro
1 seeded fresh jalapeño chili pepper, minced*
Salt and freshly ground pepper to taste

ABOUT 3 CUPS

Fresh Peach Salsa

INGREDIENTS

5 ripe peaches, peeled, pitted and cut
  into 1-inch cubes
3 ripe tomatoes, cut into 1-inch cubes
1 small bunch fresh cilantro, finely
  chopped
Half of a red onion, diced
Juice from 1 fresh lime
3 tablespoons vegetable or olive oil
Salt and black pepper to taste

ABOUT 3 CUPS

1 Stir all ingredients in a glass serving bowl; let stand 10 minutes.
  Adjust seasoning if needed. Serve. Refrigerate leftovers.

This is a tasty condiment for chicken.

White Wine Sauce

1 Heat a small skillet over medium-high heat. Coat pan with cooking spray.

2 Add onion; cook and stir 2 minutes. Stir in broth, wine and vinegar; bring to a boil. Cook until mixture is reduced to ¼ cup. Remove from heat. Stir in butter and chives. Refrigerate leftovers.

Delicious over warm chicken breast halves.

INGREDIENTS

⅓ cup finely chopped yellow onion
½ cup fat-free chicken broth
¼ cup dry white wine
2 tablespoons white wine vinegar
2 tablespoons butter
2 teaspoons finely chopped
   fresh chives

MAKES ¼ CUP

Tangy Mustard Sauce

INGREDIENTS

2 teaspoons olive oil
2 minced garlic cloves
¼ cup dry white wine
¼ cup chicken broth
2 tablespoons maple syrup
2 tablespoons Dijon mustard
¾ teaspoon chopped fresh rosemary
½ teaspoon freshly ground black
  pepper

MAKES ¼ CUP

1 Heat olive oil in a small skillet over medium-high heat. Add garlic; stir and cook 30 seconds. Stir in wine, broth, syrup and mustard. Bring to a boil. Cook, stirring constantly, until mixture is reduced to ¼ cup, about 5 minutes. Stir in rosemary and pepper. Serve warm. Refrigerate leftovers.

Serve over warm, sliced chicken.

Remoulade Sauce

1 Place all ingredients in a blender container or food processor work bowl fitted with a steel knife blade. Process until blended but not smooth. Store in the refrigerator.

Drizzle warm slices of chicken with this zesty sauce.

¼ cup hot and spicy mustard
¼ cup honey mustard
1½ cups mayonnaise
1 cup ketchup
1 hard boiled egg
2 tablespoons chopped celery
2 tablespoons chopped yellow onion
1 tablespoon capers
1 tablespoon anchovy paste

MAKES 3½ CUPS

Basil Aioli

INGREDIENTS

¾ cup mayonnaise
⅓ cup minced fresh basil
1 tablespoon fresh lemon juice
2 large cloves garlic, minced

MAKES 1 CUP

1 Mix all ingredients in a medium bowl until well blended. Cover and chill well before serving. Store in the refrigerator.

A delicious sauce to serve with chicken.

Tangerine Honey Chipotle Glaze

1 Bring tangerine juice, honey and soy sauce to a boil in a heavy medium-sized saucepan; boil until mixture is reduced to ⅔ cup, about 20 minutes. Remove from heat. Stir in grated peel and chipotle chiles. Refrigerate leftovers.

Serve over warm chicken.

INGREDIENTS

2 cups fresh tangerine juice
5 tablespoons honey
¼ cup soy sauce
2 tablespoons finely grated tangerine peel or orange peel
2 teaspoons canned minced chipotle chiles in adobo sauce

MAKES ⅔ CUP

Index

About the Author

Theresa Millang is a popular and versatile cookbook author. She has written successful cookbooks on muffins, brownies, pies, cookies, cheesecake, casseroles and several on Cajun cooking. She has cooked on television and contributed many recipes to food articles throughout the U.S.A.

Theresa's Other Cookbooks

I Love Cheesecake

I Love Pies You Don't Bake

The Muffins Are Coming

The Cookies Are Coming

The Brownies Are Coming

Roux Roux Roux

Theresa's Other Current Cookbooks

The Best of Cajun-Creole Recipes

The Best of Chili Recipes

The Great Minnesota Hot Dish

The Joy of Apples

The Joy of Blueberries

The Joy of Cherries

The Joy of Cranberries

The Joy of Peaches

The Joy of Raspberries

The Joy of Rhubarb

The Joy of Strawberries